Modesty in Dress

BOOKS BY
James Laver

An Inquiry into
the Fundamentals
of Fashion

MODESTY
IN DRESS

James Laver

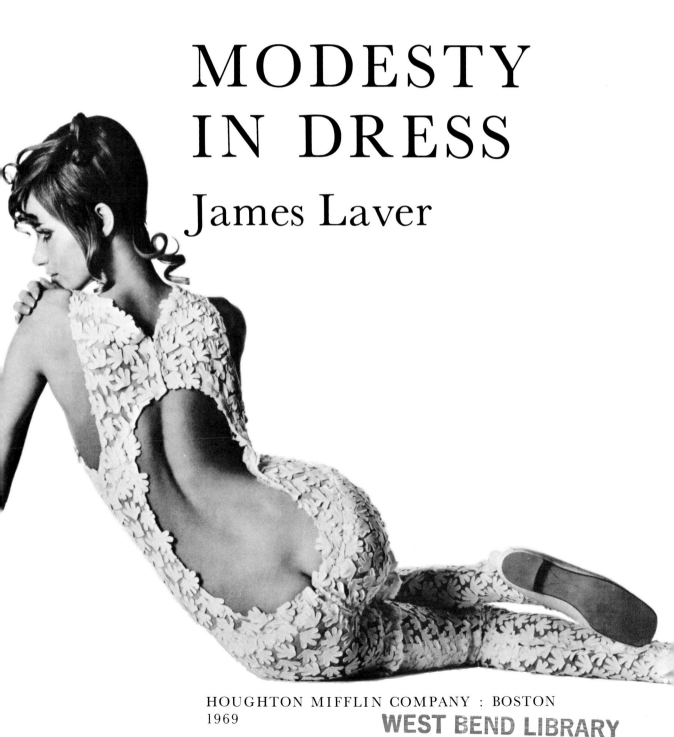

HOUGHTON MIFFLIN COMPANY : BOSTON
1969

Library of Congress Catalog Card Number: 70-77687
Printed in the United States of America

Contents

To Sir Basil Liddell Hart
Expert in More Fields than One

Modesty and its Foes

1 Until quite recently—less than a hundred years ago, perhaps—it was almost universally agreed that the primal and fundamental reason for wearing clothes was modesty. For those who accepted the literal truth of the Genesis story there was no question about it. Adam and Eve, having eaten of the fruit of the Tree of Knowledge, 'knew that they were naked' and made themselves 'aprons' of fig leaves. What need for any further inquiry into the matter?

So long as this attitude persisted there seemed no reason for defining modesty or trying to understand the mode of its operation. With the rise, however, of anthropology and psychology, it became plain that so simple-seeming a thing as modesty was, in fact, extremely complex. But before we consider this we must dispose of other theories which have been advanced for the wearing of clothes.

The most obvious is the 'common-sense' view that people began to wear clothes because they were cold. Yet the early civilizations arose in hot climates; and even before this, there is no evidence, says Ernest Crawley, 'that the approach of a glacier epoch inaugurated the invention of dress'.[1] And in modern times it has been noted that the natives of Tierra del Fuego, although they suffer much from the cold, have never invented clothes in the accepted sense. They merely have a kind of shield made of hide which they shift round to the windward side.

To the primitive mind the obvious protection against the weather was not a suit of clothes but a cave or a house. Even today the Eskimo strips naked as soon as he enters his igloo. Primitive people certainly did not wear clothes to protect themselves from the rain. A Japanese boatman will take off

[1]Ernest Crawley. *Dress, Drinks and Drums*. London, 1931.

his clothes when it begins to rain and store them in a dry place ready to put on again when the rain is over. Protection from the sun probably played a more important part in the evolution of clothes. The discovery that the shade of a tree could be made portable by the simple experiment of carrying away a branch or a large leaf would quickly lead to the invention of the umbrella and the hat. But neither of these are clothes in the strict sense.

It has been pointed out that if protection had been the dominant idea in the invention of clothing the feet and ankles would have been protected first. Some kind of moccasin, in fact, would have preceded the loin-cloth. Why, if it was not for modesty, did people begin to tie things round their middle? Some anthropologists have attempted to answer this question by what is known as the ligature-hypothesis. Nearly all the primitive peoples that have survived into our own day wear some kind of string round the middle of the body and it was supposed that its original purpose was that of an abdominal belt, useful both as a muscle ligature and to alleviate the pangs of hunger. But other writers have pointed out that the earliest girdles are merely strings, and string is useless for such purposes. The waist string is chiefly worn by men and, being made of some kind of pliant bough or stem, it is not tight enough to act as a ligature. What primitive man early discovered was that such a waist string could be used to hang things from: a weapon or a pouch—the ancestor of all pockets. Certainly, it was a great advantage in hunting and in war to have, so to speak, some ammunition in reserve, even if the ammunition in question was only a stone.

Primitive man, however, had not only to protect himself against the elements, wild animals and human enemies. In his eyes, it was even more important to protect himself against hostile magic. This motive is so remote from our conceptions that considerable effort of imagination is needed in order to understand it at all; but it seems certain that our remote ancestors were dominated all their lives by the fear of spirits and witchcraft, in particular that form of malevolent magic known as the evil eye. They feared that a mere look from an evilly disposed person might strike them with disease or weakness. Most of all they were afraid of being afflicted with sterility— in primitive thought, apart from dying of hunger, the greatest

2

possible misfortune. This danger could be averted by the use of amulets, objects selected for the most part for their supposed resemblance to the sexual parts. Most important of these was the cowrie shell, and its prestige is explained by G. Elliot Smith in the following terms:

> If the loss of blood was the first only recognizable cause of death, the act of birth was clearly the only process of life giving. The portal by which a child entered the world was regarded, therefore, not only as the channel of birth but the actual giver of life. The large Red Sea cowrie shells, which closely resembled this 'giver of life', then came to be endowed by the popular imagination with the same power.

Such shells have been found among the prized possessions of primitive people all over the world, even in places far distant from their places of origin. Cowries from the Indian Ocean were discovered in a prehistoric burial in France.

The cowrie shell, being so potent a protection against sterility, was naturally hung as near as possible to the organs of reproduction, and so girdles and aprons of these shells were worn before the idea of clothing, as such, had arisen at all. With the advent of clothes, these, and other amulets, shrank to the position of decoration or 'jewellery'. A delight in decoration was, of course, always present, even before clothes were invented. It had a life-enhancing value, and it is often difficult to distinguish protection magic from the impulse of vanity. A necklace of the teeth of tigers or other strong beasts was both an amulet and an ornament. The difficulty which primitive man found in distinguishing the motives which led him to wear such things has been aptly summarized by Hilaire Hiler:

> Suppose a bear's tooth to be worn by an individual as an indication of his prowess as a hunter, purely from the standpoint of trophyism; this would automatically suggest his ability as a food provider and thus indirectly at least would prove attractive sexually, but a bear's tooth is not without aesthetic allure from the standpoint of colour and lustre. Furthermore, it is an article which is sufficiently difficult to possess to recommend display from the point of view of its rarity. Its association with the bear, a powerful animal and worthy adversary, might imply that some quality, as strength, adherent in the bear, should persist in the tooth— fetishism and magic. If a man owned a great number of these teeth it might be assumed that he had one or all of these qualities to a superior degree thus giving significance to ornament as a mark

3

of caste. By the same token, being powerful, it would be a protector of superior quality.[1]

Hiler adds the interesting footnote that *imitation* teeth and shells, carved in ivory, were manufactured as early as the Magdalenian Period.

It is obvious that the wearing of such trophies (mixed as the motives for doing so may have been) marked a man out from his fellows. Even such a simple act as sticking a feather in the hair had social implications, for if a man stuck in too many he was likely to provoke the jealousy of the other men of the tribe; he had to fight to defend his right to wear them, with the result that only the most successful fighters were able to have feathers in any number. This can be seen to this day (or until very recently) among American Indians, where the Big Chief wore a whole crown of feathers and the simple braves but one. It came to be taken for granted that the Chief was *entitled* to more decoration than the ordinary warriors and in time the system crystallized, first into an unwritten sumptuary law and then into the insignia of rank. This is the Hierarchical Principle which still makes it seem natural that the red band round the hat of the general is out of place round the hat of the private. There is an element of class-consciousness in the very earliest developments of male attire. Even the most humble member of the community, however, decorated himself in some way. No man, it would seem, is too primitive to take delight in, one cannot as yet say, 'dressing himself up' but in 'dolling himself up', if the phrase may be permitted. 'The savages known to science', says Crawley, 'are, as a rule, very fond of finery, absolutely, and not always in relation to the other sex. The natural man will undergo any trouble, any discomfort, in order to beautify himself to the best of his power.' And this is true even when there is no question of clothes. The Brazilians of the forests of the Amazon possess no clothing in the ordinary sense, the men wearing merely a string round the lower abdomen, to which the women add a small strip of bark cloth. The blackfellow of Central Australia wears a similar string to which is attached a pubic tassel, yet all these people are fond of ornament and on special occasions wear a great deal of it, even if sometimes the 'ornament' is simply a question of painting the body.

[1]Hilaire Hiler. *From Nudity to Raiment*. London, 1929.

4

South Australian Aborigine mother
and child (from *Die Frauenkleidung* by
C. H. Stratz).

Mohammedan lady of Tunis (from
Die Frauenkleidung by C. H. Stratz).

Sir E. F. Im Thurn describes the toilet of a Guiana Indian:

He coats both of his feet up to the ankles with a crust of red; his whole trunk he sometimes stains uniformly with blue-black, more rarely with red, or he covers it with an intricate pattern of lines of either colour; he puts a streak of red along the bridge of his nose; where his eyebrows were until he pulled them out, he puts two red lines; at the top of the arch of his forehead he puts a big lump of red paint, and probably he scatters other spots and lines somewhere on his face.

Beau Brummell himself could hardly have taken more trouble.

What does all this do for a man? To speak of an inherent aesthetic sense is perhaps to beg the question. What seems certain is that the practice of decorating the body, either by painting it or tattooing it or by wearing decorative adjuncts of any kind including clothes, is that it is life-enhancing.

The most vigorous exponent of the theory that the main motive for wearing clothes was an attempted enhancement of the personality was Lawrence Langner. Langner approached the problem from a different angle from that of most writers who have concerned themselves with the history of dress. He was much occupied with the drama, being Director of Theater Guild of New York. He therefore knew a great deal about 'dressing up'; but he was also professionally concerned with scientific patents, and he tended to regard clothes as inventions to satisfy not only material but spiritual needs.

Starting with Carlyle's dictum that 'the first spiritual want of a barbarous man is decoration', and putting aside what might (by a gross over-simplification) be regarded as the Freudian view, he bases himself solidly on the teaching of Alfred Adler, that 'we can best understand the manifold and diverse movements of the psyche as soon as our most general pre-supposition is recognized, viz: that the psyche has as its objective the goal of superiority'. Adler continues:

Whether a person desires to be an artist, the first in his profession, or a tyrant in his home, to hold converse with God, or humiliate other people, whether he regards suffering as the most important thing in the world to which everyone must show obeisance, whether he is chasing after unattainable ideals or old deities, overstepping all limits and norms, at every part of his way he is guided and spurred on by his longing for superiority, the thought of his God-likeness, his belief in his special magical power.

6

This is the text on which Langner bases the exposition of his own theory:

> Man from the earliest times has worn clothes to overcome his feeling of inferiority and to achieve a conviction of his superiority to the rest of creation, including members of his own family and tribe, and to win admiration and to assure himself that he 'belongs'. . . . Whatever may have been the various reasons which led man to invent clothes, the results of wearing them soon began to appear. One of these was the self-importance which clothing imparted to man in the wearing and the pleasure he derived from this, as well as the admiration he derived from his fellow men. Furthermore he was able to cover his body and particularly his sexual and excretory organs for protection and thus to hide these parts from himself and others. . . . When man began to seek explanations for the mysterious, unknown and frightening phenomena of nature, such as thunder, lightning, earthquakes and especially nightmare, illness and death, he invented the answers in the form of ghosts or spirits and finally gods, who appeared in dreams and often seemed to have powers greater than his own. He created these gods in his own image and endowed them with most of his virtues and many of his vices. . . . Then, paradoxically enough, man sought to propitiate or control these gods and to emulate their virtues. In this he was helped by the invention of clothes which covered his body, kept his higher centres plainly visible but covered the lower centres which advertised his kinship to the animal world. He no longer felt akin to this animal world but to the world of gods or spirits.[1]

Even today, people hate to be reminded of their kinship with the animal world. Hence the rage and disgust which a century ago greeted the publication of Darwin's *The Origin of Species*. Langner suggested that human pubic hair was a distasteful reminder to human beings that they too were, vestigially at least, fur-bearing animals; and it is interesting to note that when the present author tried to have Langner's book brought out in England, a leading London publisher rejected it on the grounds that this idea would be quite unacceptable to the reading public.

We arrive, therefore, at the paradoxical conclusion that the primary reason for wearing clothes was not modesty but its opposite, i.e. self-aggrandizement. Flügel, writing as a psychologist (incidentally one of the few professional psychologists who have concerned themselves seriously with the question

[1] L. Langner. *The Importance of Wearing Clothes*. New York, 1959.

7

of clothes) accepts the anthropologists' view that decoration is the primary impulse and modesty 'something that is secondary'. It is a reaction against a more primitive tendency to self-display and, therefore, seems to imply the previous existence of this latter, without which it can have no *raison d'être*. He points out that display and modesty are opposed to one another:

> The essential purpose of decoration is to beautify the bodily appearance so as to attract the admiring glances of others and fortify one's self-esteem. The essential purpose of modesty, if indeed not the exact contrary, is at least utterly opposed to this. Modesty tends to make us hide such bodily excellences as we may have and generally refrain from drawing the attention of others to ourselves. Complete simultaneous satisfaction of the two tendencies seems to be a logical impossibility. . . . This is, I think, the most fundamental fact in the whole psychology of clothing. It implies that our attitude towards clothes is *ab initio* 'ambivalent', to use the invaluable term which has been introduced into psychology by the psycho-analysts; we are trying to satisfy two contradictory tendencies by means of our clothes, and we therefore tend to regard clothes from two incompatible points of view—on the one hand, as a means of displaying our attractions; on the other hand, as a means of hiding our shame. Clothes, in fact, as articles devised for the satisfaction of human needs are essentially in the nature of a compromise; they are an ingenious device for the establishment of some degree of harmony between conflicting interests. In this respect the discovery, or at any rate the use, of clothes, seems, in its psychological aspects, to resemble the process whereby a neurotic symptom is developed. Neurotic symptoms, as it is the great merit of psycho-analysis to have shown, are also something of a compromise, due to the interplay of conflicting and largely unconscious impulses. Some symptoms of this kind seem indeed to serve as a compromise between almost exactly the same tendencies as those which find expression in clothes. Thus the attacks of psychological blushing from which some patients suffer are, on the one hand, exaggerations of the normal symptoms of shame, but on the other hand, as psycho-analytical examinations demonstrated, at the same time involuntarily draw attention to the sufferer and thus gratify his unconscious exhibitionism. In terms of this very close analogy it may indeed be said that clothes resemble a perpetual blush upon the surface of humanity.[1]

In one of its aspects modesty is a check on the impulse to self-aggrandizement, an inhibition of 'dressing up'. But modesty

[1] J. C. Flügel. *The Psychology of Clothes*. London, 1930.

8

has another aspect: 'the attempt to damp down sexual allure'. This, of course, is the sense in which the word modesty is generally used, and it goes without saying that the term is usually applied to women. The modest woman is one who does not exploit any of the available devices for drawing attention to her sexual attractions. In Flügel's words:

> The impulses of modesty may be aroused either by a predominantly sexual or a predominantly social situation, though the sexual and social elements are both present as a rule in some degree. No doubt the sexual is the more important of the two, and, in European civilisations at any rate, operates almost exclusively to the exposure of the naked body.

This is not true of other cultures. The Australian Aborigine is indifferent to his own nakedness but is deeply ashamed if he is seen eating. He does not apparently feel shame or even embarrassment if he is seen defecating. Modesty, in fact, can be quite independent of clothing, for as Havelock Ellis observes, 'many races which go absolutely naked possess a highly developed sense of modesty'. And Im Thurn, who made a detailed study of the Indians of Guiana, was convinced that modesty is 'in its origins independent of clothing. . . . Physiological modesty takes precedence of anatomical modesty; and the primary factors of modesty were probably developed long before the discovery of either ornaments or garments.'

Even if exposure of part of the body causes shame, it is not always the same part. European travellers in the Middle East have often noted that an Arab peasant woman caught in the fields without her veil will throw her skirt over her head, thereby exposing what, to the Western mind, is a much more embarrassing part of her anatomy. In pre-revolutionary China it was considered shameful for a woman to show her foot. In Japan the same was true of the back of a woman's neck, and in other countries the knees, the navel, the finger tips and other seemingly innocent parts of the female body have been regarded in the same way. In such a sophisticated society as that of eighteenth-century France, while deep décolletage was allowed, it was considered improper to expose the point of the shoulder.

The feeling of shame may be aroused even when there is no question of 'exposure' at all. E. Adamson Hoebel quotes the case of:

> Baron von Nordenskiold, in his Amazonian travels, undertook

9

to purchase the plugs (i.e. the large cylindrical wooden plugs worn in the pierced ear lobes and lower lips) of a Botocudo woman, who stood all unabashed in customary nudity before him. Only irresistible offers of trade goods at long last tempted her to remove and hand over her labrets (i.e. plugs). When thus stripped of her proper raiment, she fled in shame and confusion into the jungle.[1]

It would seem that the 'immodest' is simply the unusual. As the same writer puts it:

The sense of modesty is merely a habit, not an instinct. The discomfiture that is felt when one's sense of modesty is disturbed is a diffused neuro-physiological upset of a large part of the nervous and organic system, shock-stimulated by a behaviour situation that contrasts sharply with those to which a person has been intensely habituated. And, of course, there is more than the element of mere habit in the total situation. There has also been a strong ideational indoctrination that penalties, social or supernatural, accompany any departure from the habituated pattern. Apprehension of dire consequences contributes much of the tone to fear and anxiety that colours the feeling of immodesty.

Psychologists have sought a real distinction between shame and guilt and some have even maintained that human societies are divided into those which are 'shame-conscious' and those which are 'guilt-conscious'. Freud maintained that guilt, or self-reproach, is based on an internalization of values, mostly parental values, whereas shame is based on the disapproval of others, but he admits that guilt can easily become shame if other persons know about it.

Ruth Benedict follows the same line, but later writers have considered the distinction too simple, and have contrasted instead the feeling of wrong-doing and the feeling of inferiority. Gerhart Piers declares that 'whereas guilt is generated wherever a boundary . . . is touched and transgressed, shame occurs where a goal . . . is not being reached . . . guilt anxiety accompanies transgression; shame failure'. But even this is too simple. The authors of Genesis certainly implied the 'guilt' of Adam and Eve at having transgressed God's law, but what they attributed to them was shame—at their own nakedness. In short, guilt and shame frequently overlap. What we are concerned with in this study of modesty is shame, if only we can isolate it and relate it to the wearing of clothes.

It is curious that the root-meaning of shame in the Germanic

[1] In M. E. Roach & J. B. Eicher. *Dress, Adornment, and the Social Order.* New York, 1965.

10

languages is 'to cover up'. English and German have only one word for shame, in one's own eyes and in the eyes of others; French distinguishes between *pudeur* and *honte*. *Pudeur* is what saves you from the danger of *honte*; *pudeur* in fact, is modesty.

As Helen Merrell Lynd points out: 'Throughout our Western civilization shame is related to the uncovering of nakedness. The terms *Sham* and *Schamgefühl* in German carry the implication of uncovered nudity, and *Sham* is part of the compound words referring particularly to the genitals.'

Paradoxically, it is the custom in some savage societies to remove articles of dress as a mark of respect, and this, Flügel suggests, is because, in such societies, 'relative or absolute nakedness is often a sign of inferior social status, subserviency or submission; while there tends to be a positive correspondence between social rank and quantity of garments worn'. Survivals among civilized people are the removal of the hat among Europeans and the removal of the shoes among Moslems. The feeling that nudity, especially the nudity of women, is in some way shameful, seems to have been most marked among the Semites. Neither the Ancient Egyptians nor the Ancient Greeks appear to have had this feeling to any marked degree. The bas-reliefs of Nineveh have only to be compared with Egyptian wall paintings and Greek sculpture to make this plain.

Some earlier anthropologists were inclined to believe that it was male jealousy which endowed women with clothes. They pointed out that in some primitive communities it was the *married* woman who was clothed in order to conceal her body from other men's eyes, the unmarried girl being allowed to run about almost naked. But this situation does not arise in the stage of savagery, but in the stage of barbarism when woman has become man's property. The ultimate term of this use of clothing as concealment is reached with the veiled women of Islam. It is, in short, a comparatively sophisticated notion of the purpose of costume, a notion which could never have arisen in really primitive communities and cannot therefore be used as an explanation of the origin of dress.

So, when dress had been invented, and women were first allowed, and then compelled, to wear clothes, the essential ambivalence of human reactions to clothing soon began to make itself felt. In Langner's words:

Greek sculpture of the fifth century B.C. showing the lightly draped figure of Aphrodite.

11

Instead of reducing man's sexual desires, it actually increased them. Mankind, striving to rise above the call of the flesh, became one of the most erotic of all living creature because of his clothing. . . . Man appears to be one of the few creatures among the higher mammals of which the female, as well as the male, . . . maintains an interest in sexual activity spring, summer, fall and winter, and morning, noon and night.

So the French *philosophe* was justified in maintaining that man was distinguished from the animal creation by drinking when he wasn't thirsty and making love all the year round. Without clothing, man would perhaps have remained *seasonal* in his erotic impulses, and although, by atavism, it is still in the spring that 'a young man's fancy lightly turns to thoughts of love', he persists in his love-making for the whole twelve months. It would be unfortunate, in modern conditions, if he did not. The mind boggles at the thought of maternity hospitals crammed to capacity at Christmas time and empty for the rest of the year.

Anatole France makes play with the idea that clothing the female can increase erotic desire in an amusing and well-known passage in *L'Île des Pingouins*. A missionary saint insists that the female penguins, since they have been converted to Christianity and therefore privileged to share '*la malédiction d'Ève*', must be clothed. One young female, as an experiment, is therefore dressed, with the result that she is chased by the male penguins all over the island. She has learnt the meaning of modesty, and, as France maliciously adds: '*Il est certain que la pudeur communique aux femmes un attrait invincible.*' Certainly those who have studied the habits of primitive peoples in modern times have been forced to accept similar conclusions. E. B. Hurlock notes that 'when primitive peoples are unaccustomed to wearing clothing, putting it on for the first time does not decrease their immorality, as the ladies of missionary societies think it will. It has just the opposite effect. It draws attention to the body, especially for those parts of it which are covered for the first time.'[1] Many anthropologists would support this view and would add that, when habitually naked tribes do wear clothes, they do so for the express purpose of increasing sexual stimulation, as in fertility dances and the rites of spring. But the whole question of 'dressing up to dance' must be left to a later chapter.

[1] E. B. Hurlock. *The Psychology of Dress*. New York, 1929.

12

Pharaoh Akhnaton and Queen Ne titi (about 1365 B.C.) wear ample revealing costumes (photograph M sell Collection).

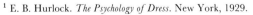

As soon as we try to understand psychological motivation, we inevitably enter the world of ambivalence. In dealing with modesty, for instance, we often find the same phenomenon evokes both desire and disgust. When the bikini first appeared on European beaches, it undoubtedly produced erotic emotions in younger men. Some of the older men and nearly all the older women were disgusted; and their disgust seems to have been quite genuine. We even hear of people being made 'physically ill' by what seemed to them an excessive amount of bare flesh.

We may sum up by saying that modesty is an inhibitory impulse directed against either social or sexual forms of display. It is opposed both to the wearing of gorgeous clothes, and to the wearing of too few clothes. It aims on the one hand at the prevention of desire or satisfaction (social or sexual), and on the other at the prevention of disgust, shame, or disapproval.

It is the enemy therefore (if the crudity of such terms may be allowed) of Swagger and Seduction. Now, historically, it is the female who offends modesty by seduction and the male who offends modesty by swagger. The 'lust of the eye and the pride of life' have always evoked the disapproval of moralists. It is the story of their efforts, in the name of modesty, to fight against both of these which must be considered in the next chapter.

Assyrian marble relief of the ninth century B.C. showing King Asshurnazipal with a Court official (photograph Mansell Collection).

13

The Lust of the Eye and the Pride of Life

2 Modern writers on dress, unlike their predecessors who liked to dilate on 'the follies of fashion', have come to the conclusion that clothes are never a frivolity: they always mean something, and that something is to a large extent outside the control of our conscious minds. It would seem, in fact, that our clothes are dictated to us by the deepest unconscious desires of the opposite sex. Throughout the greater part of history and prehistory, men have chosen their partners in life by their attractiveness as women. Therefore, women's clothes are intended to make their wearers as attractive, as women, as possible. Women, on the other hand, have, for the greater part of human history, instinctively chosen their husbands for their capacities to maintain and protect a family. Of course, this is an extreme simplification of the problem but it is a useful guide to the two principles which may be said to govern respectively male and female dress. Women's clothes are governed by what might be called the Seduction Principle, that is, they are sex-conscious clothes. Men's clothes, on the other hand, are governed by the Hierarchical Principle, that is, they are class-conscious clothes. Balancing these two principles is the Utility Principle, that is, wearing clothes as a protection against the elements, but this principle, except in extremely cold climates, has had singularly little influence on the history of costume. In general, the purpose of clothes for women has been to make them more sexually attractive and the purpose of men's clothes has been to enhance their social status. The whole ascetic and Puritan position is a protest against the use of clothing for these purposes. In moralist terminology the Seduction Principle is 'the lust of the eye', and the Hierarchical Principle is 'the pride of life'. Both are unsparingly condemned.

This condemnation begins very early. The prophet Isaiah

14

Minoan image of a goddess or prie
c. 1500 B.C. (Mansell Collection)

had no doubt of the wickedness of women who tried to make themselves attractive:

> Moreover the Lord saith, Because the daughters of Zion are haughty, and walk with stretched forth necks and wanton eyes, walking and mincing as they go, and making a tinkling with their feet: Therefore the Lord will smite with a scab the crown of the head of the daughters of Zion, and the Lord will discover their secret parts. In that day the Lord will take away the bravery of their tinkling ornaments about their feet, and their cauls, and their round tires like the moon, the chains, and the bracelets, and the mufflers, the bonnets, and the ornaments of the legs, and the headbands, and the tablets, and the earrings, the rings, and nose jewels, the changeable suits of apparel, and the mantles, and the wimples, and the crisping pins, the glasses, and the fine linen, and the hoods, and the vails. And it shall come to pass, that instead of a sweet smell there shall be a stink; and instead of a girdle a rent; and instead of well set hair baldness; and instead of a stomacher a girding of sackcloth; and burning instead of beauty.

This Semitic attitude (although it was not confined to the Semites) was adopted by the early Christians to explain their own position. But Ernest Crawley makes the interesting suggestion that their reaction to the luxury and vice of Imperial Rome was due not merely to this but to their own class consciousness, to their pride in lower-class conditions of simplicity and poverty. They felt so strongly about this that we find in early Christian literature, notably in the *Acts of Perpetua and Felicitas*, stories of willingness to endure torture rather than put on what were regarded as 'idolatrous' garments. This preference for lower-class clothes can be paralleled in recent times, as with the *sans-culottes* of the French Revolution, the peasant's and workman's blouse adopted by the Bolsheviks and, in an extreme form, in the hostility shown by the Red Guards of modern China against any form of 'bourgeois' dress.

Even cleanliness came to be condemned, although there is a curious ambivalence in the early Christian attitude. On the one hand, we have the Biblical suggestion to 'keep yourselves unspotted from the world' and the claim that there were not only 'saints in Cæsar's household' but 'white garments even in Sardis'. Clean clothes, therefore, were a symbol of purity. On the other hand, extreme asceticism often condemned cleanliness as a danger to the spiritual life, and the great St Jerome

15

16   'The Lust of the Eye' (engraving a portrait of Lady Blessington by Thomas Lawrence).

himself approved the observation that 'the purity of the body and its garments means the impurity of the soul'.

This attitude has been rightly condemned as 'a biological perversion and a social danger', but of course from one point of view it is logical enough. Personal cleanliness makes the body more sexually attractive and therefore promotes the lust of the eye. Clothes can only be kept clean by a certain amount of wealth and leisure. They are therefore a status symbol and so tend to promote the pride of life.

The distinction between the clean upper classes and what the Victorians called 'the Great Unwashed' persisted almost until our own day, and can still be detected in such a phrase as 'the white-collar workers'. Cleanliness at wrist and throat (that is to say, the two places where linen can most easily be dirtied) is still a sign that the wearer does not engage in any kind of 'degrading' manual toil.

Early Christianity placed great emphasis on the opposition between body and soul. The ideal of *mens sana in corpore sano* was repudiated. St Paul's words, 'I keep under my body and bring it into subjection', were the starting point for the body hatred of the early ascetics. This hatred was, of course, particularly directed against the female body and indeed against woman herself. James Donaldson remarks very pertinently that 'What the early Christians did was to strike the male out of the definition of man, and human being out of the definition of woman. Man was a human being made for the highest and noblest purposes; woman was a female made to serve only one.'[1]

Clement of Alexandria declares that a woman should feel 'shame even to reflect of what nature she is'; and the great Tertullian in his pathological hatred of women becomes quite hysterical in his invective:

> Do you not know that each one of you is an Eve? The sentence of God on this sex of yours lives in this age; the guilt must of necessity live too. You are the Devil's gate-way; you are the unsealer of that forbidden tree; you are the first deserter of the divine law; you are she who persuaded him whom the Devil was not valiant enough to attack; you destroyed so easily God's image, man. On account of your desert, that is death, even the Son of God had to die.

This attitude was shared by such revered fathers of the Church

---

[1] James Donaldson. *Woman: her position and influence in Ancient Greece and Rome and among the Early Christians*. London, 1907.

as Cyprian and Commodian, and the translator of the ante-Nicene Fathers into English confesses that the language used of women was so obscene that he was compelled to leave certain passages in the original tongue.

Tertullian would not allow even 'natural grace' in a woman. It must, he said, 'be obliterated by concealment and negligence, as being dangerous to the glances of the beholders' eyes'. Clement of Alexandria declared that a woman should be clothed from head to foot when she went abroad and that even her face should be hidden. This was especially necessary in church for 'If thus with modesty and with a veil, she covereth her own eyes, she shall neither be misled herself, nor shall she draw others by the exposure of her face, into the dangerous path of sin. For this willeth the Lord, seeing that it is meet for the woman that she pray with covered head.'

That this ascetic hatred of the body was a neurosis is evident by its result: the diversion of interest in the body to what was supposed to inhibit its sexual attractiveness, i.e. dress. One might even call it the beginning of fetishism. Therefore 'a new effort of modesty was needed to combat this fresh manifestation of the tendencies to which modesty is opposed; and thus it came about that disapproval on the part of ecclesiastical authority was expressed almost as vigorously as the disapproval of the cult of the body itself'.

Two woodcuts from the Elizabethan *Roxburgh Ballads*.

The clothes recommended, of course, were to be as plain as possible and undyed, for dye, says Commodian, 'is unnecessary for health, afflicts greedy eyes, and, moreover, it is false, for God would have made the sheep purple if He had wished the woollen clothes to be purple'. The same author condemns all ornaments for 'it is not right in God that a faithful Christian woman should be adorned'. And Cyprian in his work on *The Clothing of Virgins* says: 'Let your countenance remain in you incorrupt, your neck unadorned . . . let not rings be made in your ears, nor the precious chains of bracelets and necklaces encircle your arms or your neck; let your feet be free from golden bands, your hair stained from no dye, your eyes worthy of beholding God.'

Perhaps it is not surprising that all early Christian virgins were not willing to accept so austere a standard and 'for this reason therefore,' says Cyprian, 'the Church frequently mourns over her virgins'.

18

Even Christian virgins, except those who had deliberately adopted the celibate life, wanted to find husbands, and they must have found, as women have found throughout the ages, that even concealment can be used as a means of attracting the male. We are compelled, in fact, to agree with Dr Willett Cunnington's malicious comment that:

> We have to thank the Early Fathers for having, albeit unwittingly, established a mode of thinking from which men and women have developed an art which has supplied them with so much agreeable entertainment, so many satisfying substitutes for Nature's omissions, and so many novel means of exciting the sexual appetite. Prudery, it seems, provides mankind with endless aphrodisiacs; hence, no doubt, the reluctance to abandon it.

In general, however, the clothes of most people must have been so uncouth that even the most austere moralist could have found little to complain about. But in the early Middle Ages the extravagance—and the sermons—began again. One would gather from the strictures of the early thirteenth century that everybody was clad in silk and cloth of gold and adorned with jewellery and embroidery of the most lavish kind. This of course was not so, but it is certainly true that the upper classes clad themselves as gorgeously as they could, and one of the effects of the Crusades was to make them more gorgeous still by opening up trade with the East. Silks, brocades, damasks (the very word damask is an indication of where such materials originally came from, i.e. Damascus) became available to those who could afford them. Even before this we find that the wife of a knight might have quite an extensive wardrobe if we may judge by the twelfth-century manuscript in which a knightly widower admonishes his daughters not to be like their mother. In a dream he had seen St Michael and the Devil weighing the good deeds of the dead lady against her sins. In one scale were her charities, in the other her costly clothes. The Devil says: 'This woman you claim had ten diverse coats, and as many gowns; half would have been sufficient; and with the value of one of these gowns no less than forty poor men could have been clothed and kept from the cold, and the mere waste cloth in them would have saved two or three from death. She is evidently mine.' St Michael is compelled to confess himself beaten and the lady's soul is carried off to Hell.

It will be noted that what the writer of the manuscript was

The 'hierarchical' ruff (Queen Elizabeth I, National Portrait Gallery, London).

The 'compromise' ruff (Queen Elizabeth I, by Federico Zuccaro).

19

complaining about was the richness of the clothes; there is no question of their seductiveness, and indeed, at this period, European women were almost as completely wrapped up as their oriental sisters. Décolletage and other weapons of fashion had not yet been invented—or reinvented. Clothes were still largely regarded as an assertion of social status. The growing wealth of cities and the emergence of a prosperous trading class, wealth without any corresponding status, faced the aristocracy with a new problem: how to prevent the wealthy bourgeois (and the wealthy bourgeoise) from dressing as gorgeously as they did themselves. The answer was to get the government of the day to enact sumptuary laws.

There was nothing new in this. The Oppian Law of the Ancient Persians had tried to limit the number of colours in female dress and similar laws had been promulgated under the Roman Republic and the Empire. Now, in the Middle Ages, the authorities tried again. In France in 1292, Philippe le Bel issued a law regulating the number of dresses, and the value of the materials of which they were to be made, for each different class of society, and these regulations are curious and significant:

> Neither man nor woman of the bourgeoisie was to wear *vair*, or *gris* or ermines, nor were they allowed gold or precious stones or coronets of gold or silver. The ladies of Dukes, of Earls, or of Barons of 6,000 livres of land or more might have four new robes a year and no more. The same regulation applied to the other sex. Knights, and of course their ladies, were allowed two robes a year, either by gift, or purchase, or otherwise. No damoiselle, unless she were a châtelaine, or a lady of 2,000 livres of land, was to have more than one robe a year. Limits were also to be placed on the value of materials. The wives of Barons were not to have a robe of material worth more, according to the value in Paris, than 25 sols tournois a yard; the wives of bannerets and châtelains were limited to 18 sols a yard; and the wives of bourgeois of the worth of 2,000 livres tournois or more were limited to 16 sols a yard; and the poorer class to 12 sols.[1]

Similar attempts were made by the Emperor Frederick II and the English Kings Edward II and Edward III. Edward IV of England tried to regulate the clothing of all ranks of society, and so, in the following century, did Henry VIII and Queen Elizabeth, neither of whom was noted for the sobriety of their costume.

'The Pride of Life' (King Henry V by Holbein).

[1] T. Wright. *Womankind in Western Europe.* 1869.

20

Modesty in Dress

This attitude received a good deal of support from moralists who objected on religious grounds to all finery but felt compelled to make some exception in the case of the upper classes. Even the sour Puritan Philip Stubbs, writing in the reign of Elizabeth, feels constrained to add to his diatribes against vanity in dress the following significant passage:

> I doubt not but that it is lawful for the nobilitie, the gentrie and the magisterie to wear rich attire, every one in their calling. The nobilitie and gentrie to ennoble, garnish and set forth their birthes, dignataries and estates. The magistries to dignify their callings, and to demonstrate the excellencie, the majestie and worthinesse of their offices and functions, thereby to strike a terrour and feare into the hartes of the people, to offend against their office and authority . . . and as for private subjects, it is not at any hande lawful that they should wear silkes, velvets, satens, damaskes, gold, silver, and what they list (though they be never so able to maintain it), except, they beyng in some kinde of office in the Commonwealth, do use it for the dignifying and innobling of the same . . . but now there is suche a confused mingle-mangle of apparell and such preposterous excesse thereof, as anyone is permitted to flaunt it out in what apparell he lusteth himself, or can get by any kind of meanes, so that it is very hard to know who is noble, who is worshipful, who is a gentleman, who is not; for you should have those who are neither of the nobilitie, gentrie, nor yeomanrie, no, nor yet any magistrate nor officer in the Commonwealth, go daiely in silkes, velvets, satens, damasks, taffeties and suche like; notwithstanding that they be both base by birthe, meane by estate, and servile by callyng, and this is compte a greate confusion and a generall disorder in a Christian Commonwealth.[1]

The Gorgeous Male, 1480 and 162?

In all this we hear little of the Seduction Principle, and Philip Stubbs seems much more concerned with the excessive elaboration of female dress than with the often extreme décolletage fashionable in his day. However, we find a hint of it in a sermon preached by his contemporary, Bishop Hall. In this he complains not only of the elaboration of a woman's clothes when she is seen from behind, but of their shamelessness when seen from the front. He speaks of 'A powdered frizzle, a painted hide shadowed with a fan not more painted, breasts displayed, and a loose lock swung wantonly over her shoulders betwixt a painted cloth and a skin'.

This religious and moralist puritanism gave place towards

[1] Philip Stubbs. *The Anatomie of Abuses*. London, 1583.

22

the middle of the seventeenth century to something which might be called economic puritanism. In essence this was a protest against the purchase of foreign finery rather than an objection to luxury as such. However, several edicts were launched in the reign of Louis XIII in France to compel people to wear collars of plain linen without the addition of expensive lace. The effect of this was of short duration for it was seen that if the nobility were clothed too plainly home manufacture of luxury goods would suffer. Perhaps the sumptuary laws of this period should be regarded less as moral prohibitions than as an attempt to deal with the balance of payments problem. There is a curious paucity of reference to immodesty in dress in the sense of exposure of the person. It was not indeed until the end of the eighteenth century that the flimsy and diaphanous gowns of the *Directoire* provoked the anger of the moralists. At the same period protests against extravagances in dress faded out just as clothes of one half of humanity, at least, went plain and remained so for nearly a century.

However, in the period following the *Restauration* of the Bourbons women's clothes became gorgeous again and those who objected to them took up the theme of economic puritanism. But it was not until the very end of the century that Thorsten Veblen made an all-out assault on the whole basis of what he called 'the pecuniary culture'. In his epoch-making book, *The Theory of the Leisure Class*, first published in 1899, he maintains that the whole of historic civilization is motivated by three related things: Conspicuous Consumption, Conspicuous Leisure, and Conspicuous Waste.

The general application of the theory need not for the moment concern us but he devotes a whole chapter to 'Dress, as an Expression of the Pecuniary Culture', which has a considerable bearing on the subjects we are discussing.

> No line of consumption [he says] affords a more apt illustration than expenditure on dress . . . Other methods of putting one's pecuniary standing in evidence serve their ends effectually, and other methods are in vogue always and everywhere, but expenditure on dress has this advantage over most other methods, that our apparel is always in evidence and affords an indication of our pecuniary standing to all observers at the first glance. It is also true that admitted expenditure for display is more obviously present

23

and is, perhaps, more universally practised in the matter of dress than in any other line of consumption. . . . It is true of dress in even a higher degree than most other items of consumption, that people will undergo a very considerable degree of privation in the comforts or necessaries in order to afford what is considered a decent amount of wasteful consumption; so that it is by no means an uncommon occurrence, in an inclement climate, for people to go ill clad in order to appear well dressed. . . . Simple conspicuous waste of goods is effective and gratifying as far as it goes; it is good *prima facie* evidence of pecuniary success, and consequently *prima facie* evidence of social worth. But dress has subtler and more far-reaching possibilities than this crude, first-hand evidence of wasteful consumption only. If, in addition to showing that the wearer can consume freely and uneconomically, it can also be shown in the same stroke that he or she is not under the necessity of earning a livelihood, the evidence of social worth is enhanced in a very considerable degree. Our dress, therefore, in order to serve its purpose effectively, should not only be expensive but it should also make plain to all observers that the wearer is not engaged in any kind of productive labour. . . . Elegant dress serves its purpose of elegance not only in that it is expensive but also because it is the insignia of leisure. It not only shows that the wearer is able to consume a relatively large value, but it argues at the same time that he consumes without producing.

He then goes on to deal, in a perhaps not wholly satisfactory manner, with the phenomenon of fashion. He confesses that no satisfactory explanation had hitherto been offered of this, but concludes that:

This principle of novelty is another corollary under the law of conspicuous waste. Obviously, if each garment is permitted to serve for but a brief term, and if none of last season's apparel is carried over and made further use of during the present season, the wasteful expenditure on dress is greatly increased. . . . The changing styles are the expression of a restless search for something which should commend itself to our aesthetic sense; but as each innovation is subject to the selective action of the norm of conspicuous waste, the range within which innovation can take place is somewhat restricted. . . . In point of practical fact, the norm of conspicuous waste is incompatible with the requirement that dress should be beautiful or becoming. . . . The substantial futility [of fashionable dress] forces itself so boldly upon our attention as to become unbearable, that we take refuge in a new style. But the new style must conform to the requirement of reputable wastefulness and futility. Its futility presently becomes as odious as that

24

Clothes in which no man can work (
Du Maurier, *c.* 1880).

of its predecessor. The only remedy which the law of waste allows us is to seek relief in some new construction, equally futile and equally untenable. Hence the essential ugliness and the unceasing change of fashionable attire.

Oscar Wilde summed it up very neatly when he said: 'After all, what is fashion? It is usually a form of ugliness so intolerable that we have to alter it every six months.'

Since Veblen's day women's dress has become noticeably less elaborate, but the fashionable woman does not (or did not until recently) spend less on her wardrobe than her mother during *la belle Epoque*. For what she was buying now was *priority*, so that the 'model dress', that is the dress which had a head start before the copies began to filter down, became ever more expensive.

That this was Conspicuous Waste is obvious; but it was a much more difficult target for the moralist to hit than the extremely elaborate dresses of former ages. Indeed, after the First World War, as after the French Revolution, women's dress became extremely plain, so plain indeed that they could hardly be cited as exemplifying the Pride of Life. The charge therefore swung back to an attack on dress as exemplifying the Lust of the Eye and the curious spectacle was witnessed of an attempt yet once more to bring in sumptuary laws. This was most obvious in America, for Americans have always tended to believe that people could be made good by legislation. In the early '20s, in the State of Utah, a bill was promoted providing fines and imprisonment for those women who wore on the streets 'skirts higher than three inches above the ankle'. In Virginia it was proposed to forbid any woman to wear blouses or evening gowns which displayed 'more than three inches of her throat'. Ohio was even more severe, limiting the décolletage to two inches, and the same State legislature was asked in addition to prevent the sale of any 'garment which unduly displays or accentuates the lines of the female figure' and to prohibit any 'female over fourteen years of age' from wearing 'a skirt which does not reach to that part of the foot known as the instep'.

However, to the horror of all right-thinking people, the hem line continued to rise, and the Archbishop of Naples committed himself to the statement that the recent earthquake at Amalfi was due to the anger of God against the shortness of women's

Crinolines (by Leech, 1858).

GOODWOOD RACES.—CHRISTENING THE CUP.

'Conspicuous Consumption' (f
Sporting and Dramatic, 1875).

26

skirts. It is really a rather astonishing fact of social history that all sumptuary laws are always ineffective. State and Church, and Puritan moralists of all shades of opinion, have tried to control fashion and all their efforts have ended in failure. In general they have given up the attempt, unless it be argued that the clothes rationing of World War II was a kind of sumptuary law. But even in this case the authorities were defeated, for when Christian Dior's New Look was launched in 1947 Sir Stafford Cripps and the Board of Trade, as we shall see in a later chapter, did their utmost to persuade women not to wear it. It was all in vain. It would seem that so far as clothes are concerned, the Lust of the Eye and the Pride of Life will continue to exercise their ancient sway.

3 The world today is so much obsessed with the idea of Fashion, it accepts so unquestioningly the notion that women's clothes should change every season, that we have to make an effort to realize that, in the long perspective of history, Fashion is quite a modern invention.

However far we go back in time or far away in space, we find tribes, however primitive, who have some form of dressing up, even if they only do it on special occasions, such as the spring fertility festival. But such dressing up has nothing to do with Fashion in our sense.

Among the Ancient Greeks, the only women who wore fine clothes and adopted new modes were the *hetaerae* who, in spite of their social prestige, were outside the pale of respectability. For respectable women the rule was to look as inconspicuous as possible and to veil before the world those charms which were reserved for the husbands only. The Christian ethic reinforced this tendency, with the result that during the next thirteen centuries there was hardly any change in women's clothes at all.

Then, in a single generation, everything changed. In the fourteenth century there was a sudden realization that clothes, instead of mere wrappings, could be used to attract the attention, and influence the choice, of the other sex; and in little more than a decade were invented the three devices on which Fashion has played infinite variations ever since: tight-lacing, décolletage and striking head-dresses.

Instead of the main garment being loose and enveloping, it was cut to reveal the shape of the figure and, in particular, the smallness of the waist. Corsets had not yet been invented but the dress was stiffened to give very much the same effect. And, instead of the dress concealing the throat, it was cut away to reveal much of the bosom.

28

How 'Fashio. Operat

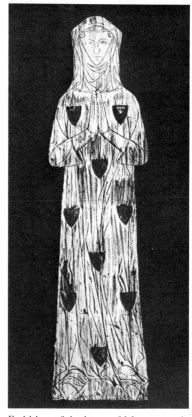

How 'Fashion' Operates

Décolletage, indeed, had been discovered to be the most potent weapon in the feminine armoury and it can be plainly seen where one would least expect it: on a sepulchral monument. In actual life, as we know from contemporary records, it was carried to much more daring lengths, sometimes involving the complete exposure of the breasts. Even when only the neck and throat were exposed, this was so daring a departure from the doctrine of modesty which the Church had so long imposed, that it could only mean that a new spirit was in the air. Décolletage is as much a sign of the first dawn of the Renaissance as the novels of Boccaccio. Life was opening like a flower, and clothes were responding with a symbolic gesture, as they always do.

The new head-dresses showed a similar spirit of liberation, for instead of the veil being used to conceal the hair and a considerable portion of the face, it was drawn away from the countenance with pins and wires, and even attached like a flag of revolt to towering constructions in the shape of a church steeple or the devil's horns. All the fantasies of the milliners of later ages can be seen, in embryo, in these points and peaks of curiously folded cloth, if it is not misleading to call such plainly diaphanous veilings cloth—veilings which concealed nothing but spread themselves aloft, as fragile as the wings of butterflies.

The revolution—for it was a real revolution—happened in the luxurious courts of France and Burgundy and, if we have to couple the innovation with any particular name, we could probably choose none better than that of Isabeau, or Isabelle, of Bavaria, who married the French King, Charles VI, in 1385. She had extravagant tastes and at once began a career of luxury and lavish expenditure which helped to bring the country and the monarchy to ruin. It was one succession of fêtes and masquerades, and one is tempted to think that some of the extraordinary fashions of the late fourteenth century began as the costumes of a fancy-dress ball.

Fashion, in order to operate, needs a platform for display, a theatre, as it were, in which to perform, and this was provided by the Court. It also needs a certain degree of female emancipation, for women must be free to compete for male attention: in this case the attention of the king. So the king's mistresses might be considered to share the dictatorship of Fashion with the queen herself.

Rubbing of the brass of Margarete de Camoys in Trotton Church, Sussex, *c.* 1310.

The Birth of 'Fashion'

Rubbing of the brass of A. Cheyne in Hever Church, Kent, 1419.

29

Elizabeth Hasylden, *c.* 1480 (L
Chesterford Church, Essex).

But Court costume has always tended to formalize, and even to fossilize, itself into insignia of rank; and to prevent this from happening it is necessary that there should be an ambitious and prosperous bourgeoisie, aping the manners of the aristocracy and copying their clothes, in spite of all the sumptuary laws enacted to keep them in their place. Of course Fashion had for a long time little effect on the dress of the common people, but by the beginning of the fifteenth century, if not earlier, it is safe to say that every woman who could afford it knew what Fashion was and followed it as best she could.

Such an event, such an acceptance of change, is the beginning of modernity. It is the emergence of the mobile modern world from the static world of the early Middle Ages. It is the victory of Time over Place, for no longer did people dress according to their nationality or even according to their position in society, but according to the *year*. Today the process is almost complete, so that we can no longer say that is a Spanish dress, or a French dress, or an English dress, but only that it is a dress of such-and-such a year. The 'Time-disease' has now infected the whole world; its first symptoms can be detected about the year 1350.

There is therefore a particular interest in studying the dresses of the early centuries of Fashion and watching how they were gradually developed. How do we know about such things? What evidence have we that Fashion really did begin about the middle of the fourteenth century? There were no fashion plates at that period, no engravings even. There were a few pictures, but these were almost all devoted to religious subjects. There are a few sculptures which seem to show contemporary dress, but they cannot be relied upon as an exact record. Anything like a continuous, yearly sequence of fashion is extremely hard to come by, or rather, it would be but for a source of information which has only just begun to be exploited.

This source consists of what are called brass-rubbings. In southern England and in the Low Countries (and curiously enough, nowhere else) the usual monument in churches from about 1250 to 1620 was a brass, that is to say a fairly thin sheet of metal incised with a design, usually a human figure, and cut round to form a kind of silhouette. This was let into a slab of stone cut to receive it, and was then used as a grave-stone,

31

in the floor, or on the wall, of a church. There is no question of bas-relief; stone and metal plate form a perfectly flat surface, and from this surface, with its clean incisions, a rubbing can be taken with great ease.

Brasses have the enormous advantage of being almost all dated, and although one must allow for a time-lag, especially in the remoter parts of the country, it is at least possible to say that any given fashion must have been in existence on the date given, even if it first appeared a few years earlier.

A collection of several thousand of such rubbings is preserved in the Victoria and Albert Museum, and is well-known to students, especially to students of armour, for it goes without saying that many, if not most, of the male figures are shown in all the panoply of war. But, for study purposes, brass-rubbings have certain disadvantages. Many of them are exceedingly large, and the predominance of black makes a very gloomy effect. Then, too, it is very difficult for the eye to understand a *negative*, which is what the brass-rubbing inevitably is. However, if selected brass-rubbings are photographed to make them more or less uniform in size, and if they are then re-photographed from the negative, a new world is opened. It is like coming across a whole collection of line-drawings, all clear and comprehensible, and some of them of great beauty. In a recent exhibition it was found possible to provide an almost continuous series from 1377 to 1648, and what struck most of those who went to see them was the *modernity* of some of the dresses; and, strangely enough, it was the earlier examples which looked more modern than those of later date. There is nothing in modern fashion which suggests the farthingales or the gigantic ruffs of the Age of Elizabeth; nothing corresponding to those hieratic forms, stiff with embroidery and loaded with jewels. But some of the fashions of the late fifteenth century might, with very slight modifications, have been designed today.

There is the same feeling for slim elegance, the same physical type even; the fall of the skirt is that of a modern evening gown; and some of the head-dresses bear the oddest resemblance to modern hats. What little jewellery is worn is worn in the modern manner; even some of the faces are more in accordance with modern taste than most of the faces of intervening periods.

32

Courts long continued to dominate Fashion, and from the beginning of the sixteenth century we can gain all the information we need, no longer from sepulchral monuments, but from the multiplicity of portraits in oil. We have ample evidence, for example, of what Queen Elizabeth I looked like, and so many engravings were made of her portraits that it was not difficult for her subjects to dress like her—if they could afford it. Anne of Denmark, Queen of King James I, was also a leader of fashion, and with the arrival of Henrietta-Maria as the wife of Charles I, French influences began to permeate English modes.

The influence of Courts, however, was not all on one side. They provided a platform for Fashion but they were also rooted by their nature in the Hierarchical Principle. It is possible to study the conflict and the interaction of the two tendencies over several centuries, and the resultant forms of dress which emerged. One example may suffice. The great ruffs of the second half of the sixteenth century are obvious examples of the Hierarchical (anti-Utility) Principle. In men this principle was complete and the ruff a perfect round. But women were governed also by the Seduction Principle (i.e. they wanted to take advantage of décolletage) and so the ruff was broken to allow the bosom to be exposed. The ruffs worn by the ladies of the Court of Elizabeth show this curious compromise.

Whether the Hierarchical Principle or the Seduction Principle ruled at any given Court depended largely upon the personal character of the monarch. At austere Courts like that of Spain, hierarchy became almost fossilized, with the result that the Court costumes of 1600 remained unmodified almost throughout the century. When Louis XIV met his Spanish bride she was still wearing a farthingale. But at Louis's own Court the Seduction Principle had won the day, since it was always possible that any lady might attract the favour of the monarch.

Spain, indeed, by the end of the seventeenth century had fallen behind in prestige and influence. A hundred years earlier hers had been the dominating influence even in countries like England which were politically hostile. But now France took over and until the French Revolution it came to be more and more accepted throughout Europe that 'fashionable'

Forty years of hem-lines.

opposite page 1927
above 1949

page 37 1967: The mini-skirt at Ascot (*The Daily Telegraph*).

clothes, both for men and women, were French clothes.

The French hegemony was assisted by the rise of a new means of disseminating fashion. Following in the wake of Abraham Bosse, whose delightful engravings of social life give such a convincing picture of the dress of the upper classes in the reign of Louis XIII, there arose a whole school of print-makers producing what were not actually fashion plates but pictures which could be used as such. They were essentially *after the event* in the sense that they were based on clothes actually worn at the French Court. The prints of artists like Jean de Saint-Jean and the Bonnarts showed single figures with such titles as 'Lady of Quality in Winter Dress' and 'Lady in Summer Déshabille' and, being easily transportable, did much to increase the dominance of French modes.

In the eighteenth century another method of dissemination was adopted by Rose Bertin, the celebrated dressmaker of Marie-Antoinette. She dressed dolls in the latest Court fashions, packed them into a huge coach and travelled with them all over Europe. It is needless to say that they were eagerly purchased.

The same period showed a spectacular increase in print-making in this field and the beginnings of what can only be described as fashion journalism. Early in 1778 two Parisian print-sellers, Jacques Esnauts and Michel Rapilly, began to issue a regular series of etchings, coloured by hand, and representing the prevailing male and female fashions. The 'Galerie des Modes et des Costumes Français Dessinés d'après Nature' is a magnificent production, its only rival being Heideloff's 'Gallery of Fashion', which first appeared in 1794. That this was published in London was due to the fact that Heideloff, a German born in Stuttgart in 1761 who had migrated to Paris in the 1780s, was driven thence by the Terror. Soon there was a spate of fashion plates and fashion magazines on both sides of the Channel, and *le dernier cri* came within the reach of every woman.

The next development was the rise of the male couturier, the first and most famous of them being Worth. In spite of the fact that he was an Englishman and never learned French properly, he had, ten years after his arrival in Paris in the early 1850s, established himself as a veritable 'dictator of fashion'. His innovation consisted in the fact that he did not deign to

34

visit his clients in their homes: he expected them to come to him, and even then he did not accept them unless they came armed with suitable introductions. He was a real creator and some of his original designs have been preserved.[1] Being no draughtsman, he had made a series of lithographed heads and arms and on these he drew his creations. His success led other couturiers to follow in his wake so that, whereas in 1850 there were only 158 of them in Paris, by the end of the century there were more than 1,500.

The role of the creative couturier has been much debated. What kind of man is he, and how does he maintain his power (if indeed he has any such power except in details) to 'dictate' fashion? It has often been noted that many male couturiers have a strong feminine streak—and inversely, that those few women dress designers who have reached the top of their profession, have a noticeable touch of masculinity. On this observation Edmund Bergler builds an entire theory of the unconscious motives of the male couturier in designing women's clothes.

> The normally heterosexual male [he says] protects himself against women with the hoax of the He-man. The homosexual has no equivalent armour. He protects himself with self-delusion, claiming that he is 'indifferent' to women; he protects himself with malicious pseudo-aggression, expressed in a variety of ways, all covering his masochistic regression. If he happens to be a fashion designer, he encircles his sphere of legitimate conduct with a shady borderland that is suffused with *unconsciously* illegitimate and malicious intentions. This is the homosexual's fashion-hoax.[2]

To summarize Bergler's elaborate theory, perhaps not quite justly, the homosexual designer's 'unconscious defensive hatred of women' leads him to design for them deliberately ugly clothes. He rejoices when, at his instigation, they make themselves ridiculous.

One cannot help wondering if this is entirely true even on the unconscious plane. Perhaps it is not the *extreme* type of homosexual who becomes a dress designer. The psychologists have now convinced all of us that very few men (if any) are

---

[1] On the closure in Paris of the House of Worth-Paquin, the present writer, then Keeper of Prints and Drawings at the Victoria and Albert Museum, was able to secure a collection of some twenty thousand original designs for dresses, some going back to the early 1860s. These can now be consulted in the Department.

[2] Edmund Bergler. *Fashion and the Unconscious.* New York, 1953.

35

100 per cent male and very few women 100 per cent female. We are all, to some extent, both male and female: it is all a question of degree. The successful dress designer is one who has enough of the woman in him to understand what it is all about and enough of the man to stand, as it were, two paces back and see what he is doing. When the young Worth dressed dolls with scraps of material picked up during his employment at Swan & Edgar's, he was surely not doing it to spite women but to please the woman in him. Like women, he 'adored' *chiffons*.

To be dressed by Worth was, of course, immensely expensive. The Empress Eugénie could afford it and so could Princess Metternich and other ladies of her Court. So could the wives of the financiers who flourished so exceedingly under the Second Empire. But there was another class of woman who could afford it even more easily. These were the *grandes cocottes* whose rich and aristocratic lovers could deny them nothing, and whose elaborate *toilettes* were at once the delight and scandal of Paris as they drove every day in the Bois or displayed themselves in the theatre boxes or on the racecourse. It was they who now began to dominate the mode, especially after the departure of Napoleon III. Eugénie was perhaps the last royal personage to influence fashion; after her, the power passed to other hands. So we are almost back once more in a situation similar to that of Ancient Greece where the *hetaerae* were the only leaders of fashion and the Seduction Principle reigned supreme.

Many attempts have been made to decide in what this Seduction Principle really consists and why, when once a fashion has been achieved which is universally acknowledged as attractive, it should ever change. Various answers have been proposed. It was once thought that the natural frivolity and inconstancy of the female sex was a sufficient explanation. The hard-headed view was that a group of astute business men deliberately set out to 'change the fashion' and thus to induce foolish women to throw away the clothes they had bought last year and buy new ones. This opinion is still sometimes advanced but as an explanation of *why* fashions change it is plainly inadequate.

The psychologists, notably Professor J. C. Flügel, have elaborated the theory of the 'Shifting Erogenous Zone', and this,

36

Mini-skirt at Ascot, 1967 (*The Daily Telegraph*).

indeed, would seem to throw a flood of light on processes which would otherwise remain obscure. The truth seems to be that *in imagination* the whole female body is a desirable object. In practice this is not so, as anyone can testify who has ever visited a nudist camp. Complete nudity is anti-erotic, as soon as the shock of novelty has worn off; and it does wear off, surprisingly quickly. If complete nudity were common we should probably become seasonal in our impulses, like the animals. Our characteristic *permanent* eroticism is kept alive by clothes.

But clothes can only keep it alive by continually altering the emphasis, drawing attention to all aspects of the female body in turn by exposure, semi-concealment or by other devices well known to every dress designer. This altering of emphasis is the 'Shifting Erogenous Zone' and is the whole basis of Fashion.

The theory has been taken up and (as some would think) pushed to an extreme of elaboration, by Edmund Bergler:

Stripped to its essentials fashion is no more than a series of permutations of seven given themes, each theme being a part of the female body: the breasts (neckline), waist (abdomen), hips, buttocks, legs, arms and length (or circumference) of the body itself. Organs 'appear' and 'disappear' as the theme of fashion changes, and one and then another part of the body is emphasized by succeeding styles. Thus breasts and legs are 'opposites' in fashion; if in one season, the neckline plunges and breasts consequently become the centre of attraction, one can be sure that in subsequent seasons breasts will be covered and the spotlight will be on legs. And so on, in endless variations.

37

This is acutely observed and if one must enter a *caveat* it is merely that the two emphases may occasionally overlap. If we take film stars as the reigning embodiments of the erotic ideal we can see that the thoracic development of actresses like Martine Carol and Gina Lollobrigida still continued to attract after the advent of short skirts in 1956. In justice to Bergler, however, we should also note the gradual replacement of the Lollobrigida type by actresses like Audrey Hepburn which has occurred during the last decade.

Fashion is essentially a game of hide-and-seek between seduction and prudery, and nothing is more astonishing than the things prudery finds itself able to accept, once it has grown used to them. Once a particular emphasis has been established, no one feels well-dressed without it. A woman of 1860 who was *not* wearing a crinoline felt slightly indecent; and the same was true of the exaggerated posterior of the bustle period and the flat chest of the '20s.

Sometimes prudery seems to be winning and sometimes seduction; if either were ever completely victorious Fashion, as we know it, would simply cease to exist. As we have noted, the fifteenth century was, in western Europe, a period of considerable erotic emphasis notable for pinched-in waists and low-cut

Jumpsuit by Ungaro. 'The cu gives a certain deliciousness to small of the back.' (Penn photogr from *Vogue*. Copyright © 1967 Condé Nast Publications Inc.).

38

bodices. By contrast, the clothes of women in the early Tudor period seem almost prudish, but a few years later it was far otherwise. Queen Elizabeth I was extremely décolleté all her life and the fashion persisted into the next century.

In the middle of the seventeenth century, the Puritan domination both in England and America brought in a more modest style of dress; but with the Restoration of Charles II, modesty, and even decency, was thrown to the winds. The Lely portraits at Hampton Court show us a series of 'Court beauties' who certainly wear their clothes in no prudish spirit; although perhaps we should add that Lely's paintings are nearly all, to some extent, 'fancy portraits', and not conclusive evidence of the clothes actually worn.

It was the same in France; but the ageing Louis XIV came under the influence of the pious and bigoted Madame de Maintenon and clothes assumed a new propriety. In England, writers like Addison were in plain reaction against the licence of the period of exaggerated hips and deep décolletage. Curiously enough, the eighteenth century was prudish about *shoulders*. The corsage might be cut so low that it was hardly decent without a *fichu*, but no respectable woman ever appeared in public with the point of the shoulder exposed.

The period following the French Revolution had entirely different notions. Clothes were now light and flimsy. The legs, which had been hidden for so long, were discernible underneath the gown and were sometimes actually seen, for the material of dresses was often semi-transparent, and pink tights had to be worn underneath. And it was no longer the 'cleavage' of the bosom that was visible, but its rounded forms above the ribbon-encircled high waist.

Legs had a short outing in the 1830s to vanish again in the '40s, when it became improper even to refer to them. On the other hand, early Victorian modes, which give a general impression of prudishness, allowed a straight-across décolletage for evening which would have been considered highly improper in the eighteenth century.

In the late nineteenth century and early twentieth, Fashion worked by suggestion. Skirts were long and trailing, so trailing that they had to be lifted up when walking—and when they were, they revealed a 'froth' of frilly lace petticoats. This was a period when the suggestion of underclothes was deliberately exploited.

Modesty in Dress

There was a certain décolletage in evening dress but, on the whole, the corsage was extremely proper, a neckline *up to the ears* being considered essential for day wear. It is amusing to note that when this was abandoned, the so-called V-neck which resulted was denounced from the pulpit as immoral and by medical men as likely to lead to pneumonia!

All this, however, was nothing to the horror evoked by the post-war styles of the '20s. Women were showing their legs, and it was not a mere matter of glimpsing an ankle but of being presented with the spectacle of knees. The present age, which has pushed the hem-line even higher, finds it difficult to understand the excitement this caused. Nothing like it had ever been seen before in the whole history of civilized costume. Certainly if any woman had walked out into the street in 1915 in the clothes of 1925 she would have been arrested for indecent exposure. Even in the '20s the new 'immoral' fashions were fiercely denounced, but women continued to wear them.

And then, in 1930, legs suddenly became a bore. As the psychologists say, they had 'exhausted their erotic capital', and the emphasis shifted to the back of the dress, or rather to what would have been the back of the dress if it had not been 'backless'.

Having lived through these changes, the present author endeavoured, in the late '30s, to draw up a chart.[1] This laid it down that the same dress is indecent ten years before its time, daring one year before its time, *chic* (*chic* being defined as contemporary seductiveness) *in* its time, dowdy three years after its time, hideous twenty years after its time, amusing thirty years after its time, romantic a hundred years after its time and beautiful a hundred and fifty years after its time.

The fashions of the mid-'20s were revived (in Dior's H-Line) in 1957, by which time thirty years had elapsed. The 'gap in appreciation' lasts just about one generation, and anything that falls inside that gap is 'hideous'. There are some amusing examples of this. The French fashion historian Octave Uzanne, in a book published in 1891, uses the word 'hideous' to describe what to us are the 'romantic' fashions of 1860. And Thackeray, providing his own illustrations for *Vanity Fair*, firmly refused to clothe Amelia and Becky Sharp in the 'hideous' dresses of

[1] First published in *Taste and Fashion*, Harrap, London, 1937. It has since been widely reproduced and, following the lead of the *New York Herald-Tribune*, is generally known as 'Laver's Law'.

40

1815. He calmly clothed them, in defiance of all historical accuracy, in the costume of 1840!

How does a particular fashion originate? Many people imagine that they have an easy answer to this question. A great lady has some personal peculiarity or defect: a withered arm or a scar on the neck which she wishes to hide, and the fashion designers obediently introduce a falling sleeve or a 'dog-collar' of pearls round the throat. A queen is about to give birth to a prince and to conceal her *grossesse* a hooped skirt of some kind is invented. The Empress Eugénie has often been cited as the inspirer of the crinoline, but a proper study of costume history does not support this view. There was an unbroken series of widening skirts from 1820 until 1860, and they would have gone on expanding and ultimately needing to be supported by a revived farthingale if Eugénie de Montijo had never existed.

Even when some items of clothing bear a personal name it is often doubtful whether the owner of the name was really responsible for introducing the fashion. Wellington was certainly not the inventor of Wellington boots, nor Blücher of 'Blüchers'. They merely wore, and popularized, a boot that had already arrived. The 'Duchess of Devonshire' hat, immortalized by Gainsborough, had been growing bigger and bigger for a decade on other heads than hers.

Some men, and women, are so much the children of their age that we can hardly conceive the age without them. They become, in turn, the type which is admired and copied, and whatever innovations in Fashion there may be are inevitably attributed to them. So Byron has been credited (or the reverse) with the invention of trousers. They might with as much reason have been called 'Wellingtons', for it was the great Duke himself who was refused admittance to Almack's, with its fashionable assembly, on the grounds that he was wearing trousers. He was a decade too soon; he ought to have been wearing breeches!

The lower classes had worn trousers for decades. The *sans-culottes* of the French Revolution wore them—hence the name ('without breeches'). They were also worn by Turks and other romantic people of the Near East; and their adoption for general wear was a concession to democracy on the one hand and a budding romanticism on the other. And the man who

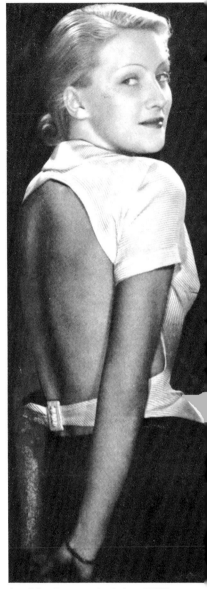

A girl photographed by Willinger (*Paris Plaisirs*).

41

summed up these two tendencies in his own person (for he was looked upon in his own day as dangerously democratic) was— Byron.

There is perhaps only one person in English history who can claim not only to have given his name to a fashion but to have invented the thing itself—albeit by accident: Lord Spencer. This eccentric nobleman, who flourished in the early years of the nineteenth century, was one day warming himself with his back to a roaring fire when the flames caught the tails of his new coat, and before help arrived they had been completely consumed. Unwilling to sacrifice a fine new coat he called for his tailor, bade him cut away the charred fragments of the tails and finish off the coat neatly without them. He then, with imperturbable sang-froid, stepped into the street and so inaugurated the fashion for tailless coats, or, as they were universally called, spencers. They became extremely fashionable and were even worn by women. In fact they lasted on women far longer than they lasted on men. Lord Spencer is the exception that proves the rule. Yet even here precursors could be found—in hussars' uniforms and schoolboys' jackets. An eccentric might bring in a tailless coat for men in 1800; a thousand Lord Spencers could not have introduced one in 1700, or even in 1750. The general lines of the accepted costume would have made it impossible.

Fashion, at least in retrospect—we cannot pass any valid judgment on the fashions of our immediate past—has a curious coherence. Even when it seems most arbitrary, as with the unconventional attire adopted in our own day by the hippies and 'flower people', it has a very close relationship to the interior decoration, and even to the architecture, of its period. More than that, it has a symbolic value, so that strait-laced epochs are strait-laced in both senses of the word, and when women are emancipated nothing will prevent them from throwing away their corsets and also from cutting off their hair.

The Prince Consort wore a black top-hat because in an era of genteel respectability he couldn't possibly have worn anything else. A tricorne would have fitted neither his head nor his soul. The early Victorian lady in short skirts, the Bright Young Thing of the 1920s in crinolines: both ideas are absurd. You cannot change about even the accessories of Fashion without putting back the clock of the universe and making

42

nonsense of history. Fashion is a very much bigger thing than individual taste or personal convenience, and the innovators of Fashion themselves are no more than corks on the stream— large and conspicuous corks sometimes, but still corks. There is something in the story of the clothes we wear which is beyond our comprehension and certainly beyond the control of our conscious minds. That is the reason of its importance and the secret of its perennial fascination.

Formalized
and Fossilized Dress

4 It is a commonplace that men's clothes, except for purely utilitarian garments such as flying-kit or dungarees, cannot be explained on any rational principles. They can only be explained historically. We can only say: the reason why such and such a garment is worn is that it is descended from another garment, worn perhaps two hundred years ago, the purpose of which was quite different. That it is with us today is due to an historical accident, or rather (since there are no accidents) to a complex of influences—sociological, economic, political, or even religious. Men's evening clothes are a case in point.

Perhaps it would be truer to say that they are *the* case in point, for a man's evening coat—the black tailcoat that is still worn on formal occasions—is the type garment, the prize exhibit, giving us, in epitome, the history of every male garment since what we know as modern dress took shape. All male garments begin by being 'sports clothes'. They then become informal day wear, then formal day wear, then evening wear. Push them a stage farther and they become the dress of servants or functionaries. The men's tailcoat has been all these things.

It was originally a hunting coat, with a square slice cut away to enable its wearer to sit a horse more comfortably. As such it was worn by the English country gentleman round about 1780. After the French Revolution rather dashing young men began to wear it in Town just as today they wear corduroy trousers and lumber jackets. Early in the nineteenth century Beau Brummell, by tightening and smartening it, made it the accepted day wear of the fashionable man. It was not yet evening wear. The tailcoat as we know it did not establish itself finally as evening wear until the eighteen-forties by which time only old-fashioned gentlemen still continued to wear it in the daytime.

Tobias Smollett by an Italian a about 1767 (National Portrait Gal London).

44

At the same period—the '40s—it went black and various theories have been put forward to explain why it did so. Some have seen an explanation in the new smokiness of the early Victorian atmosphere, but this would surely explain the darkness of day clothes rather than of those worn in the evening. And after all, smuts fall upon skirts just as surely as upon trousers. A more plausible reason, if only because it transfers the whole question to the field of psychology, is that the darkness of men's clothes at this period was due to a kind of Byronic Bulwer Lytton romanticism which willingly assumed the habiliments of woe. Bulwer Lytton himself, one of the most successful men that ever lived, delighted to look upon himself as a 'blighted being', and his influence in the world of fashion was immense.

Whatever the reason, black became the accepted hue of men's evening clothes, until in our own day a timid attempt has been made to introduce a hint of colour. The fact remains that almost any evening coat from 1840 onwards could be worn as evening dress today without its wearer looking unduly conspicuous or out of fashion.

'Full evening dress' therefore has remained practically unchanged for the last hundred years. But before we consider this extraordinary state of affairs, we are bound to ask ourselves what was worn by the fine gentleman in the evening before 'evening dress' was invented. The answer seems to be that up to the French Revolution he simply wore his grandest clothes, those of the finest silk or velvet, those covered with the greatest area of embroidery or gold lace. He also wore his finest shirt, and the finer the shirt the more likely it was to be provided with an elaborate frill concealing the buttons down the front. It was the custom to leave the upper part of the waistcoat unbuttoned in order to allow this frill to be seen. This is of the greatest importance in the development of evening dress, for it explains the characteristic low waistcoat which has been one of its most striking features ever since.

In a French print published about the year of Waterloo and showing an '*Anglais en habit habillé*', we see the shirt frill still protruding. The whole outfit indeed is one of a most interesting transitional type. Rather surprisingly, we see that the coat has not the characteristic square slice cut out of it: the type has not yet absolutely established itself. Further, we

45

A Study in Fossilization

William Congreve by Sir Godfrey Kneller, 1709 (National Portrait Gallery, London).

Sir Alexander Cockburn, Lord C Justice of England from 1859.

note that the *Anglais* in question is wearing knee-breeches, white silk stockings and eighteenth-century buckled shoes. He has abandoned the wig and the pigtail but the remains of the 'bag' are attached to the back of the coat, rather like the 'flash' on the tunic of the Royal Welch Fusiliers. A sword is still worn at the side in the eighteenth-century manner, but the hat is no longer a tricorne but a 'bicorne'. This bicorne—as being more conveniently tucked under the arm than the topper—remained in use in the ballroom at least until the 1840s.

It only really disappeared after the advent of the 'gibus', called so after its first inventor. Already in 1848 Thackeray in his *Book of Snobs* described 'the fashionablest little fellow in town' with his 'gibus-hat and his little glazed pumps'. It is curious to reflect that the hat which had originally been made in that form precisely because it was stronger and so did not collapse—it was indeed a hunting hat or primitive crash-helmet—should have imposed its shape so completely on the imagination as a necessary part of the gentleman's evening outfit and should have been made *collapsible* for his convenience in carrying it about in the crush of the opera or the ballroom.

But to return to the shirt. By the early '40s the frill no longer stuck out but was tending to be more and more flattened against the chest. By the late '40s it was completely flat but vestiges of its earlier exuberance can be seen in the folds of the shirt-front. A vestigial and meaningless one-sided serration is seen as late as the '70s. The collar was for long entirely, or almost entirely, concealed by the stock. It was only in the '50s that the stock dwindled into the bow tie.

46

It was towards the end of the same decade that another important change took place. We have seen that in the early years of the century breeches were still worn with evening dress. The victory of the trousers was fairly complete soon after Waterloo, but in evening dress they took the form of tights; that is, they preserved the shape of breeches and stockings even when they were a single garment reaching from waist to ankle. It was not until the early '60s that they became noticeably loose both in day and evening wear.

The anonymous author of *The Habits of Good Society*[1] gives us invaluable information about the state reached by men's evening clothes at the time of the Crimean War. After remarking that in America a man might go to a ball in white ducks and that in France he had the option of light grey, he lays down the English rule: 'For all evening wear—black cloth trousers.' He tells us also that 'the tail coat of today is looser and more easy than it was twenty years ago,' and admonishes his readers to 'abjure such vulgarities as silk collars, white silk linings, and so forth, which attempt to beautify this monstrosity, as a hangman might wreathe his gallows with roses. The plainer the manner in which you wear your misery the better.'

According to this mentor, the waistcoat should also be black.

In France and America, the cooler white waistcoat is admitted. We have scouted it, and left it to aldermen and shopkeepers. The only evening waistcoat for all purposes for a man of taste is one of simple black cloth, with the simplest possible buttons.

These three items never vary for dinner-party, muffin-worry or ball. The only distinction allowed is in the neck-tie. For dinner, the opera, and balls, this must be white, and the smaller the better. The black tie is only admitted for evening parties.

Such rules however were by no means universally observed. We find white waistcoats cropping up at intervals for the rest of the century, and in the twentieth century, after the First World War at any rate, white waistcoats were nearly always worn with 'full evening dress'. It is perhaps worth mentioning, as an historical note, that an elderly don at Oxford advised the present writer in 1920 to wear a black waistcoat for a formal dinner party and a white one for a dance. Strange to relate, a fashion plate in the *Tailor and Cutter* in the following year shows

[1] *The Habits of Good Society. A Handbook of Etiquette for Ladies and Gentlemen.* n.d.

a dinner-jacket with a white waistcoat and 'tails' with a black waistcoat. The general opinion is that a white waistcoat with a dinner-jacket was an innovation of the Prince of Wales.

We have mentioned the dinner-jacket. The earliest fashion plate known to the present writer is dated 1881. It has a silk-faced roll collar[1] and is worn with a *white* waistcoat and a black tie. It was worn solely *en famille* or for dining with intimate friends. It did not really make its way until the end of the century. Now, of course, as the 'smoking', it has completely ousted the tailcoat on the Continent and seems likely to do so in England. The double-breasted dinner-jacket worn with a soft shirt appeared in this country in the 1930s. The roll collar has now reappeared after a temporary eclipse.

The mould, in short, seems to be breaking up. The rigid alternative of 'tails or black tie' which was so absolute a quarter of a century ago seems to be losing its meaning. The dinner-jacket is assuming the position of formal wear, which is, after all, in tune with the inevitable development of men's clothes. Many young men today do not possess tails, and if they are still thought necessary for a particular party they are hired, or borrowed from older men.

On the other hand, there is a thirst for a return to formality, and at the same time a longing for colour. This expresses itself in the 'fancy' waistcoat and in the growing habit (*horribili dictu*) of wearing a dark wine-coloured bow tie. In the opinion of the present writer, this is a passing phase. The future seems plain: the abandonment of the tailcoat altogether and the elevation of the dinner-jacket to the status of 'full evening dress'. Now that the Court has decided that decorations may be worn with a dinner-jacket we know that the evolution is complete.

So far we have only been considering the question of *formalization* in men's dress, but there is a further stage which may, perhaps, be called 'fossilization'. This occurs when men are no longer indicating their position in society, but showing that they occupy some office or function in the State. All men's clothes tend to formalize themselves; professional men's clothes tend to fossilize themselves. The most obvious example of this is the dress of the legal profession as it has survived in Great Britain. British legal costume is indeed a prize example of that

---

[1] A *half*-silk facing on a tailcoat appears in the '60s, sometimes with a velvet collar. A fashion plate of 1881 shows a tailcoat with a roll collar.

48

'Called to the Bar', 1899, by Ralph Cleaver.

process of fossilization which is among the most astonishing phenomena of costume history.

In very early days, unfortunately, verbal descriptions are more plentiful than pictorial representations, and it is a little difficult to form any very clear notion of the clothes worn by judges and other legal figures. An effigy of the Chief Justice of the King's Bench in the reign of Edward III represents him in the ordinary costume of his day. There is an effigy of the famous Judge Gascoigne, whom modern historians will not allow to have sent 'Prince Hal' to prison, which gives us a very fair notion of the shape of the robes, but not, unfortunately, of their colour. However, from the reign of Henry VI four miniatures have come down to us, representing the Court of King's Bench, the Court of Common Pleas, the Court of Chancery and the Court of the Exchequer, and authorities on historical costume accept these as accurate representations.

If we confine our attention to the picture of the Court of King's Bench we shall find in it much that is both interesting and surprising. On the Bench sit five judges all in scarlet gowns and mantles and wearing white coifs. The history of the last-named is very curious. It was a close cap for the head, apparently of white linen, and tied with strings under the chin like a baby's nightcap. In the early thirteenth century it was worn by both sexes, and we can only agree with Planché who remarks in his *Cyclopaedia of Costume* that 'on the heads of men hunting and of knights in armour it has a most ludicrous and unpicturesque appearance'. When ordinary men had abandoned it it persisted in ecclesiastical and legal costume, and in

49

the latter exists today but in so transformed a manner as to be scarcely recognizable. By the time of Henry VI it had lost its strings and rather resembled a skull cap. In the reign of Elizabeth black coifs appear over the white ones, both being worn together. By the time of Charles II only the black was worn, and this continued until the introduction of periwigs made the old position untenable. It was then, strangely enough, transferred in vestigial form to the top of the wig.

To come back to the robes, and their colour, as shown in the miniature: there is nothing surprising in the scarlet robes worn by the judges. The regulations for their apparel in the reign of Charles I are set forth in an order issued in 1635:

> The judges in term time are to sit at Westminster in their black or violet gowns whither [whichever] they will and a hood of the same colour put over their heads, and their mantles above all, the end of their hood hanging over behind, wearing their velvet caps and coiffes of lawn, and cornered caps. The facing of their gowns, hoods, and mantles are with changeable taffata, which they must begin to wear upon Ascension Day, being the last Thursday in Easter Term, and continue those robes untill the Feast of Simon and Jude; and upon Simon and Jude's Day, the judges begin to wear their robes faced with white miniver, and so continue that facing untill Ascension Day again. Upon all holy days which fall in the term, and on hall days, the judges sit in scarlet faced with taffata, when taffata is to be worn, and with furs or miniver when furs and miniver are to be worn. When the judges go to Paul's to the sermon in term, or any other church, they ought to go in scarlet gowns.

Much more confusing is the question of the dress of serjeants at-law, or barristers, as we should call them. In the miniature we have been considering there are several serjeants 'pledynge at the barre', and all of them, to borrow the words of Planché, 'are attired in party-coloured gowns, some blue and green, the blue portion rayed or striped with white or pale yellow, hoods and tippets or capes of the same and lined with white fur, of which the edge alone is seen; others in blue and mustard-colour, rayed diagonally with double stripes of black, and one in murrey and green'.

The medieval practice, which seems so strange to us, was still in existence in the seventeenth century. An account of the making of a serjeant in 1635 tells us that, after the ceremony, 'he puts off his black, and puts on his party-coloured robe of

50

black and murrey, and hood of the same . . . and all that year he goes in his party-coloured robe, and his men in party-coloured coats, unless upon a Sunday or holy day, and then in violet with the scarlet hood'. There had in fact been some simplification or, as Planché puts it: 'some time between the reigns of Henry VI and James I a change took place in the colours of the serjeant's gowns and hoods . . . green and mustard-colour had been discarded and rayed cloth [was] no longer considered to "betoken prudence and temperance"'. The coloured robes for serjeants seem to have lasted until the reign of Queen Anne, for in her coronation procession there walked 'the Queen's younger Serjeants-at-law in scarlet gowns and caps in their hands'. Some authorities believe that purple (or more probably scarlet) robes were worn as late as the reign of George II; but Lord Chief Baron Pollock was once asked why modern barristers wear black and he replied that they went into mourning on the death of Queen Anne, and never came out.

If we are never likely to see barristers in coloured robes again, we are even less likely to see them in ruffs, although there was a time in the middle of the seventeenth century when the ruff, having been abandoned by ordinary Fashion, showed signs of becoming a distinctive mark of the legal profession. In a word, it threatened to *fossilize* round the necks of English judges and barristers as it actually did round the necks of the Lutheran clergy of the Continent.

What defeated it was another candidate for fossilization, namely, the wig. The full-bottomed periwig appeared in England, as every reader of Pepys knows, in the autumn of 1663. In his *Diary* for 2 November, he remarks: 'I heard the Duke [of York] say that he was going to wear a perriwig; and they say the King also will.' Six days later, anxious to be in the fashion, he went to church himself in a wig, 'where I found that my coming in a perriwig did not prove so strange as I was afraid [we should read, perhaps, "as I hoped"] it would for I thought that all the church would presently have cast their eyes all upon me.'

Soon it was impossible for any man with any pretensions to Fashion to be seen abroad without a full-bottomed wig. The judges adopted one too, and it was this that made the wearing of the ruff impossible. It also made impossible the wearing of the falling collar which had long replaced the ruff in civilian

51

attire. Instead, it became necessary to wear a narrower collar, rather like a bib in two halves, and this in turn shrank to the falling bands which persisted round the necks of the legal and clerical professions for so long and, in the legal profession, remain to this day.

But it is the wig which has now become the distinctive mark of the English Bench and Bar, and so strange an evolution deserves a little more comment. There is no doubt that the full-bottomed wig added enormously to the dignity and gravity of the man who wore it. Fortunately we have a remarkable number of English portraits, many of them reproduced in mezzotint, of the end of the seventeenth and the beginning of the eighteenth centuries. How noble and impressive are the great figures of this Augustan Age: Marlborough, Addison, Harley, Bolingbroke! And how much the periwig adds to the awe with which we behold them.

It is true that most men soon began to think such an encumbrance intolerable. Military men especially found the long curls reaching to the shoulders impossible. The wig would not even stay on the head during a charge, and after some of Marlborough's battles the local peasants reaped a rich harvest merely by walking over the field and gathering up the fallen periwigs. Soldiers were soon compelled to fasten the hair back in what was known as the 'Ramillies tie'. To anyone engaged in any kind of active pursuit, the full-bottomed wig was something that had to be modified sooner or later. And modified it was. As the eighteenth century progressed the wigs grew smaller and smaller. The astonishing thing is that the bulk of mankind continued to wear them at all; but they did, almost until the end of the century.

Judges, however, were in different case. Immobile on the Bench or passing in stately procession on circuit, the troubles of the soldier trying to cope with a full-bottomed wig while charging the enemy cannon left the legal luminary, in both senses of the word, unmoved. So he continued to wear it and gradually, in accordance with what seem to be the laws of costume history, it began to fossilize. The loose, tumbling curls became formal rolls; the whole outline of the structure became more rigid. It was just possible to fancy that the luxuriant *chevelure* of an Addison was a natural growth; no one could possibly mistake the wig of a modern judge for real hair.

52

The falling collar and falling bands—

Top left: Jonathan Swift by Charles Jervas (early eighteenth century; National Portrait Gallery, London).
Bottom right: The Rev. D. Moore, from a portrait by Banquiet (mid nineteenth century).
Bottom left: Richard Baxter by J. Riley (mid seventeenth century).

And now we come to the strangest part of the story. For while our judges fossilized the wig which they had worn in the reign of Queen Anne, our barristers have fossilized the wig they wore in the reign of George III. All judges therefore have a certain resemblance to Addison and all barristers have a certain resemblance to Washington. From the costume point of view they are never contemporaries for there is a gap of some sixty or seventy years between them. Yet both wigs seem to us to be singularly appropriate, and few Englishmen would wish to diminish the majesty of the Law by sweeping them away.

Most professional clothes in Western Europe fossilized in the early sixteenth century. A mayor of today is dressed exactly like a mayor of the time of Henry VIII; that is, he is wearing the clothes which would have been worn by any prosperous citizen of that time, including the furred gown and the gold chain. The academic gown is derived from the same period, but the academic hood is of earlier date. The gown of the Queen's Counsel is also early Tudor, but his wig fossilized at a later period. But neither mayors nor lawyers wear their gowns except on formal occasions. Dons at Oxford and Cambridge wear theirs more frequently, but the same tendency can be seen at work. Doctors, on the other hand, have long abandoned their formal clothes except when they are sitting in state for the presentation of degrees; that is, when they are acting in some kind of academic capacity.

In former ages it would have been quite easy to pick them out. There are late fourteenth-century miniatures which offer us a picture of members of the Faculty of Paris, showing them in full dress: square bonnet, silk violet *soutane* and red robe trimmed with ermine. This was the dress of the professors. We know that the medical students of the University of Paris wore a black robe, and when they graduated received a red one. We also know that this 'full dress' was worn not only on state occasions, formal meetings for the granting of degrees and the like, but in ordinary life, when the doctors were attending the sick. The usual practice seems to have been to receive patients in the physician's own house—to open, as we should say, a 'surgery', a misnomer sanctified by long usage. Only in extreme cases do they seem to have visited the sick and we have, fortunately, a whole series of pictures stretching over several centuries, showing the doctor in his 'surgery'.

This series of pictures shows—what indeed might have been expected—that the dress of doctors follows the general lines of development of what might be called professional costume; but already in the sixteenth century there were protests in Paris against doctors who refused to wear their gowns even for the examinations of the Faculty. *A fortiori* they were not wearing them in the ordinary course of their professional duties. Evidence for this multiplies as we reach the seventeenth century with its wealth of paintings of ordinary life. In the works of David Teniers, Adriaen van Ostade, Gerard Dou and Jan Steen, doctors are frequently depicted and they are dressed like any prosperous bourgeois of the period. When wigs came into fashion doctors wore wigs, but, unlike lawyers, they did not go on wearing them when the fashion was over. At the beginning of the eighteenth century it was impossible to distinguish the doctor in the street from any other respectable citizen. Sharp eyes might, however, have been able to divine his profession from his gold-knobbed stick.

As fashion changed so the clothes of the doctor changed, but with a natural emphasis on sobriety. In a word, doctors tended to wear black. Perhaps it is fair to say that they also tended to be a little behind the times. No one expects a learned man to be anxious to keep up with the fashion. So in our own day (at least in the childhood of the present writer) it was possible to see the doctor in his frock-coat and silk hat some years after these garments had been abandoned by most professional men. The modern physician wears a lounge suit, but he would still be looked at a little askance if he presented himself at the patient's bedside in a sports coat.

The dress of surgeons followed a similar evolution to that of the physicians but with a time-lag. They were at first regarded merely as servants, and late medieval miniatures represent them in the short clothes of an inferior social status. They began to adopt the long robe and the square cap in the middle of the seventeenth century but, of course, only on what we have called academic occasions. In the nineteenth century they wore, like the physicians, the frock coat and silk hat. They wore the frock coat even for operating, for their special white laboratory clothes had not yet come into being.

Another example of professional fossilization—and the retreat from it—can be seen in the undress of the clergy. We

55

are not here concerned with ecclesiastical *vestments*, which are an extreme form of fossilization, some of them being ultimately derived from the Court dress of Byzantium. Such garments are the dress of priests when they are officiating at the altar: they are the costumes of those who act in a religious drama. But priests, like actors, are sometimes (and, indeed, for the greater part of their lives) off the stage, as it were. When they walk about among their fellow citizens, they do not wear full canonicals; they wear another less spectacular costume which, while recognizably different from that of laymen, is not conspicuously so. In other words, there is, in all ages, a clerical undress.

The reign of Henry VIII might well serve as a starting point for, as we have noticed, it was then that the costumes of so many functionaries began to fossilize. An Anglican bishop, even today, wears the costume of a courtier of Henry VIII, but made of black material and without the highly decorated (and detachable) sleeves. He is, so to speak, in his shirt-sleeves, and in modern times the curious result has been reached that a bishop (unless he is fanatically Low Church) has three costumes: first his cope, mitre and so on, readopted from the Roman usage, second his lawn sleeves for ceremonial occasions, and third his dress of every day.

The second of these is a peculiarity of the Anglican community and goes back, of course, to the day of the Reformers, who wished to discard altogether what we might call No. 1 Dress. Once more we are back at Henry VIII. There is no essential difference between the dress of Archbishop Cranmer, in the portraits that have come down to us, and the costume worn by a modern bishop at the Lambeth Conference. Archbishop Laud, a century after Cranmer, looks slightly different, because he has adopted the contemporary ruff. An eighteenth-century bishop looks different because he wears a wig (and bishops persisted in wearing wigs long after everyone else but judges and barristers had abandoned them). But the lawn sleeves remain unchanged.

The ordinary costume of the lower clergy shows no such permanent element. There was a general notion that they should dress soberly, which meant, in practice, wearing black. Their neckwear, if we may call it so, followed the fashion of the day. But there is always a tendency for clerical dress (and

The clerical collar: The Re[v] Kingham, a Baptist minister, 1[8]

Dress of the Anglican clergy [from]
The Gentleman's Tailor Fashion [Book,]
1924).

56

indeed any dress which denotes the functionary as opposed to the private individual) to stereotype itself, and to cling to forms which the layman has discarded. Thus the falling band, so typical of the late seventeenth century, persists into the eighteenth, and even to the nineteenth, in clerical dress, in the form of two long white tabs.

At the beginning of the eighteenth century the full-bottomed wig was worn by clergy and laity alike, as can be seen clearly in the portraits of Jonathan Swift. But gradually, as the century progressed, the lay wig and the clerical wig diverged. For the clergy the accepted form became a rather close-fitting white or grey bob wig. The Archbishop of Canterbury still wore one at the coronation of Queen Victoria.

The majority of Anglican clergymen in the eighteenth century seem to have worn the cassock. Even John Wesley wore it in his peregrinations up and down the country. And that it was still in use up to the end of the century can be seen from Robert Dighton's ferocious caricature of the vicar and Moses, his clerk, summoned at an unfortunate moment from the alehouse to the church. On the other hand, the contemporary illustrators of Richardson and Sterne show that some clergymen at least had abandoned the cassock for contemporary dress (black of course), with the addition of the surviving tabs. By the beginning of the nineteenth century we can gather from Jane Austen that clergymen had begun to congratulate themselves that their dress was no different from that of 'any gentleman'.

Even when the tabs were abandoned, however, the white tie persisted, and until the victory of the modern clerical collar it would have been thought highly improper for a clergyman to appear without one. And for the rest of the century we can watch an interesting contest between the white tie and no tie at all. Both had their significance, and until quite recently it was still possible to deduce a clergyman's religious opinions from his neckwear. If you wore an ordinary collar with a white tie then you were probably Low Church and Evangelical. If you wore any version of the Roman collar you displayed your sympathy with the innovations—or the restorations—of the Oxford Movement, with its attempt to bring the Anglican Church into at least an outward conformity with the practices of Catholicism. *Punch* in the early '80s has a caricature of two

Anglican clergymen in disputation. One is High, the other is Low, and the rule we have just laid down is exemplified in both cases.

Nonconformists in general were naturally inclined to the Evangelical side, and although we find Edward Irving, the founder of the sect of Irvingites, wearing the old-fashioned falling bands in the '30s, J. Kinghorn has, at the same period, a kind of soft white stock tied in front in a small bow, and C. H. Spurgeon, in the '70s, wears an ordinary standing collar *à la Gladstone*, with a white bow-tie.

The ordinary Anglican parson wore the same, together with a frock-coat and a tall hat. The frock-coat gradually yielded, towards the end of the century, to the short jacket, and the top-hat to the flat clerical soft bowler. Waistcoats were at first cut very high with a special neck, standing up, and with a square gap in the front through which the clerical collar could be seen. Later, this gave place to a V-neck waistcoat, the space thus created being filled in with a square of silk. This was in line with Roman practice.

Even the Nonconformists followed suit, and today the vast majority of ministers of the Methodist, Congregational and Baptist communities wear the Roman collar. There has, however, within very recent years, been a reaction. Many modern clergymen found that the wearing of such a collar created a barrier between them and their flock, especially among the working classes. Those, therefore, most interested in welfare work, in running settlements and missions, sometimes discard it and wear, except when they are actually conducting services, an ordinary soft collar and tie. And the tie is a coloured one; there is no question of a return to the white tie.

In this rapid survey most attention has been given to the dress of the Anglican clergy. The costume of the Roman priest had its own evolution, and shows many minor variations in the different countries of Western Europe. The old-fashioned shovel hat, for instance, can still sometimes be seen in Spain; the short frock of the Irish priest enables one to pick him out anywhere. Some priests wear the cassock habitually and it is certainly both a practical and a dignified garment. In its Roman form it is sometimes provided with a short cape, and this mode has been adopted by a few High Anglicans also.

The undress of the clergy may not form a very important

58

part of the history of costume, but its own special development exemplifies in a most interesting way some of the rules by which all dress seems to evolve. It is by no means static. It has often been modified by fashion, and is indeed inevitably a reflection or an adaptation of lay costume. But it tends, like all professional costumes, to show a time-lag, and to have certain features—like the falling bands—which tend to persist long after they have been abandoned in lay dress. The general principle is that clerical undress tries to be dignified and gentlemanly, and yet not too remote from the clothes worn by ordinary men.

A Study in Formalization

Hunting costume, *c.* 1790.
Day dress, 1844.
Evening dress, 1870.

Perhaps we might usefully conclude this chapter with an account of the elements of fossilization in Court dress. Originally it was simply the grandest dress of the period. In the presence of the monarch, the ladies of the Court made themselves as attractive as possible, while indicating at the same time the richness of their own or their husband's estates. Men's Court dress was intended to show the wealth of its wearers, as when the great Duke of Buckingham appeared at Court with a hundred thousand pounds' worth of jewels sewn all over his doublet. Louis XIV of France was one of the greatest sticklers for the elaboration of Court dress, and especially insisted on décolletage, even, strange as it may seem, when the Court was attending Mass.

Throughout the eighteenth century Court ladies wore con-

59

temporary dress, and so of course did the men, whose embroidered coats at Versailles or St James's were only slightly more elaborate than could be seen in the fashionable haunts of Paris and London. It was not until the end of the eighteenth century that a divergence began to make itself felt between fashionable costume and Court dress. This was due in England to the strange survival of the hoop; earlier in the century hoops had been worn by every woman with any claims to fashion. About the time of the French Revolution ordinary clothes, even fashionable ones, became comparatively plain, and abandoned the hoop altogether. The hoop, however, persisted at Court with some strange results.

It was at this time, too, that Court dress, especially for women, may be said to have stereotyped itself. Plumes in the hair were worn by every fashionable woman in the 1790s: they have persisted in Court dress until recently; so have the long white gloves which came in with the new short-sleeved gowns. This is in line with the inevitable tendency to formalize itself which is shown by all official costume.

This tendency to carry over elements from an older costume is seen most strikingly in the early years of the nineteenth century. Shortly before the year 1800 women's waists left their natural position and ascended to under the armpits. This was in its way a very attractive fashion, but when a woman went to Court she was compelled to put on hoops. The result was ludicrous; the sudden swelling of the skirt started much too high up for any grace or convenience; indeed it might be said that a woman's hips were now on a level with her bust. At last George IV abolished this absurd custom. Hoops, of course, returned to Court dress in the late 1850s, but only because by now the crinoline was part of ordinary fashionable dress.

Indeed we can say that from this moment when hoops were abolished, Court dress has been once more ordinary fashionable dress, only slightly grander and provided with a train, and of course with the addition of plumes in the hair and the inevitable long white gloves. Perhaps the limit was reached in the second half of the '80s. It can be seen quite plainly in contemporary numbers of magazines like *The Queen*. For the Drawing Room held on 23 March 1886, *The Queen* magazine gives a double spread illustrating five of the most elaborate toilettes. In each case the train was between twelve and fifteen feet long.

Such extreme elaboration in Court attire persisted almost until the outbreak of the First World War, although it is true that the designers of the year 1910–11 had some difficulty in reconciling the hobble skirt of the period with the long Court train.

After the war there was such a drastic simplification in ordinary evening dress for women that it could not help being reflected, to some extent, even in the costumes worn at Their Majesties' Courts. But if the train was an absurdity when worn with a hobble skirt, it was even more so when joined to the knee-length skirts of the middle '20s. Plumes in the hair, a long train behind and a skirt down to the knees in front was a true Hottentot fashion. If people had not been completely blinded (as they always are) by contemporary Fashion, they would have seen how ridiculous such a costume was and must be.

Greater elegance was possible once long skirts for the evening had returned, and some very elegant neo-classical models were produced in the early '30s. The principle of a completely different dress for Court wear was now almost universally abandoned. In other words, women wanted to wear their Court dress again as ordinary evening dress, so kept it within the limitations of the prevailing mode.

Men's Court dress, like diplomatic costume, has some curious features carried over from the eighteenth century. According to the official handbook, Court dress (old style) consisted of a black silk velvet coat with a standing collar, with seven buttons on the right front and seven notched holes on the left—purely vestigial for the buttons were not intended to button. The cuffs had turn-backs with three notched holes and buttons. The body of the coat was lined with white silk and the skirts with black.

With this went black silk velvet breeches, with three small steel buttons and cut steel buckles at the knees. The hat was a black beaver or silk cocked hat, with a steel loop on a black silk cockade or rosette. There was a lace frill at the throat and ruffles at the wrist and, of course, a sword.

But the most interesting vestigial object in this costume was what is described as a black silk 'wig bag' attached to the coat at the back of the neck, hanging over the collar; in short, a feature similar to the flash worn by the Royal Welch Fusiliers. This object, now detached from what it once adorned, is the

61

Formalization in men's dress.

only relic of the wig worn by the eighteenth-century gentlemen.

In the new style velvet Court dress this curious style was abandoned, as well as the ruffles at wrist and throat. Instead, an evening stiff shirt and white waistcoat, with a white tie, were worn. In practice, even this has been more and more completely dislodged by the *levée* dress, which substitutes dress trousers for breeches. In short, even men's Court dress gradually accommodated itself to contemporary Fashion with a time lag which might be anything up to a hundred and fifty years.

Sports clothes and formal wear, 1878.

The Special Case of Military Uniforms

5 There is a sense in which all male costume is, or tends to become, a uniform: by which is meant not something that is worn by everyone but something that can only be worn by certain people. The most primitive savage 'dresses up' to go into battle, but this is at first not a matter of putting on clothes, but of painting the skin, especially the face, in order to make it as terrifying as possible. The chief, even at this stage, is allowed more war-paint and feathers in the hair than the ordinary brave—a distinction which was later to be systematized as insignia of rank, just as the trophies of battle were later to become campaign medals.

The object of military uniforms is sixfold: first, to enhance the manly feeling of the wearer (they are therefore essentially 'un-modest' in that they promote the Pride of Life); second, to impress and even to terrify the enemy; third, to distinguish friend from foe; fourth, to reinforce the feeling of solidarity and *esprit de corps*; fifth, to establish in plainly visible form the hierarchy of rank; and sixth, to protect the wearer without interfering with his movements.

These aims have not always been manifested to the same degree in different epochs and some of them are plainly incompatible with one another. The primitive desire to terrify the enemy only survived into modern times in such vestigial forms as the death's head on the hussar's headgear and the bare ribs of the skeleton originally painted on the warrior's body and later transformed into the froggings of his tunic.

The desire to protect the wearer was pushed to extravagant lengths in the development of armour, especially of plate armour. Activity was much restricted, to such a point in the late fifteenth century that an unhorsed knight was helpless and could not even rise from the ground without assistance. With the development of firearms even the protection offered by

Chief Yeoman Warder of the Tower of London—the second oldest uniform extant. (*British Crown copyright*).

63

armour became illusory and by the end of the sixteenth
century it had begun to shrink and, as it were, wither from the
feet upwards. A hundred years later it had dwindled to the
doubtfully useful cuirass and the purely decorative gorget.
The pictures of Marlborough and other generals of the period
in breast-plates are, of course, fancy portraits and bear no
relation to what was actually worn on the field of battle.

It is really the disappearance of armour which makes
'uniform' possible. The mail-clad medieval knights strove for
as much *difference* as possible by means of crests and coats-of-
arms, many of which have survived as proud heraldic distinc-
tions. The ordinary people when gathered into armies did not

Swiss Guards at the Vatican
oldest military uniform extant.

wear any special costume, unless they were the personal retainers of some great noble, in which case they wore some distinguishing device or livery, and it is probable that this livery is the origin of the military uniforms of ordinary soldiers.

The earliest uniforms still extant are those of the Yeoman Warders of the Tower of London ('Beefeaters') in England and those of the Papal Guards at the Vatican, i.e. the body-guards of monarchs. It is probable that English troops were first clothed by the Government (but this was, for long, quite exceptional) in the reign of Edward III, who raised a thousand men in Wales, armed them with lances and provided for each a mantle and a tunic. The Yeoman Warders were raised by Henry VII in 1485 and reorganized by Henry VIII, who gave them the costume which, with the addition of an Elizabethan ruff, they still retain.

For the army which Henry raised to repel a threatened in-vasion in the thirty-sixth year of his reign he gave explicit instructions as to how they should be clothed:

> First every man sowder to have a cote of blew clothe, after such fashion as all fotemans cotes be made here in London . . . and that the same be garded with redde clothe . . . and the best sene [i.e. the best-looking men] to be trimmed after such sort as shall please the captain to desire; provided always that noe gentleman nor other wear any manner of silk upon the garde of his cote, save only upon his left sleeve, and that no yeoman wear any manner of silk upon his said cote, nor noe gentleman nor yeoman to wear any manner of badge. Every man to provide a pair of hose for every of his men, the right hose to be all red, and the left to be blew, with one stripe of three fingers, broad red, upon the outside of his leg.

It is interesting to note this very early example of the red stripe which was to have so long a history in military uniforms. The badges prohibited were, of course, feudal badges, but they had not been banished for ever, for some of the emblems derived from feudalism (now no more than badges of locality) are to be seen to this day on the caps of British soldiers.

The men sent to Ireland by Elizabeth in 1566 had uniform coats, as also those raised in Lancashire in 1584 for the same service. They were ordered to be provided with a cassock of motley, or of 'sad green' colour or russet. It is possible that we have here an early example of protective colouring or camouflage.

65

Modesty in Dress

The difficulties which troops of this period found in distinguishing friends from foes is brought vividly before us in a passage in the memoirs of Robert Cary, Earl of Monmouth, concerning the English campaigns in Flanders under the Earl of Essex. Describing a siege operation, he remarks: 'All our attempts were against St Katherine's. . . . One night there were scaling ladders prepared and we had hope to win it by scalado. . . . We were all commanded to wear shirts above the armour (I lost many shirts that I lent that night), this was done accordingly.' This may be regarded as that curious thing, counter-camouflage. It was important that the attacking troops should be able to see one another in the darkness. The 'sad green' cassocks were therefore the equivalent of the stripes of the tiger, and the shirts the equivalent of the tail of the rabbit.

Charles I took considerable pains to bring about uniformity in the dress of his troops. In the royalist parade at Oxford in 1645, the King's Life Guards and the Queen's Life Guards wore red coats; the other regiments wore white, blue and grey. Prince Rupert had a regiment of Foot Guards in scarlet. In fact the only difference between the clothes worn by the rival armies in the English Civil War was probably in the senior ranks. General officers and staff officers wore what they pleased (as indeed they long continued to do) and it was natural that there should be more silk coats and plumed hats among the Cavaliers than among the Roundheads.

Practical and impractical military uniforms—

(a) Light horseman, *c.* 1650
(b) Officers, *c.* 1660
(c) Musketeer, *c.* 1700.

b

c

The most potent reason making for uniformity, however, was the psychological one which lay behind the whole idea of Cromwell's 'New Model' army. It was based on the discovery that the *esprit de corps* and fighting spirit of a body of troops could be vastly increased by drilling them together and by clothing them in the same garb. Another, purely utilitarian, reason was that colonels found it more profitable to buy cloth for their men in large quantities and that such bulk orders were easier to execute if the colour was constant. But this affected only the coats: the breeches continued to be any colour the wearer chose.

There is plenty of evidence to show that Cromwell's army, which, at the conclusion of the Civil War, numbered fifty thousand men in England and Ireland, was extremely well appointed. Indeed, not until modern times has any more sensible and practical dress for soldiers ever been devised. His men wore loose, baggy breeches, a coat of buffalo hide sufficiently tough to turn a sword thrust, and what was called a 'pot': a steel helmet with a back-piece to protect the neck and a vertical bar in front to prevent sword slashes at the face. At his Restoration Charles II was so much impressed by both the men and their accoutrements that many of the disbanded Cromwellian troops were immediately re-enlisted for his own service. The Coldstreamers (i.e. the regiment General Monk had raised ten years before at Coldstream on the Scottish Border) became the Coldstream Guards in 1660. The Life Guards and the Horse Guards date from the following year.

The military costume of the closing years of the seventeenth century certainly showed a decline in utility. The steel helmet was universally abandoned in favour of the large hat with feathers, cocked in various styles, until it settled down into the tricorne. This was an absurd hat for the field of battle, and it was rendered still more of an encumbrance and still more difficult to keep on the head by the huge periwig. In a charge both hat and wig were likely to be lost, leaving the head completely unprotected. Yet this absurd fashion lasted through four reigns.

It is true that modifications slowly crept in, as we have already noted. The so-called 'Ramillies tie' gradually developed into a long pigtail which, unnecessary as it was, certainly kept the hair in place. Some troops wore a thick pigtail, turned up and secured with a leather strap, leaving a knob of hair below. The higher officers merely followed civilian fashion, and were still allowed a large measure of individual fancy—one distinguished an officer largely by the richness of his apparel, not yet crystallized into definite insignia of rank. And this remained true, especially for the more wealthy militia officers, for the greater part of the eighteenth century.

There was, in any case, very little difference before the Napoleonic Wars between military and civilian dress. The three-cornered hat was worn by all soldiers who were not grenadiers. The coat and waistcoat were cut on civilian lines and the only difference in the clothing of the nether limbs was that the troops wore long buttoned gaiters. All ranks wore wigs, at least in the earlier part of the century. Later the troops wore their own hair well larded and sprinkled with white powder. The pigtail disappeared only in 1808, a decade or more after it had vanished from civilian heads.

The revolution in male attire at the end of the eighteenth century consisted in the adoption of a tightened and smartened version of country clothes (that is, hunting clothes with the skirts cut away in front and a tail behind), and in wearing a top hat (hunting attire again) in place of the tricorne. The military followed suit, except that the officers retained the cocked hat for some years, but began to fold its brims in two instead of in three. The enormous bicorne worn by Marshal Ney will come immediately to mind. Napoleon wore a smaller version, and Wellington a smaller one still: the latter wore it fore-and-aft instead of square-rig, if one may make use of naval terms when discussing military uniforms.

Infantry of the line wore a felt cap, in appearance rather like a top hat without the brim and with a brass plate in front. Officers adopted the same headgear in the Peninsular War, and during the same campaigns the breeches and long gaiters with fourteen or fifteen buttons were abandoned for trousers. This, too, was in line with the trend of civilian fashion.

So far we have been dealing only with infantry uniforms and noted that, in spite of minor divergences, they closely resembled civilian dress. It is very different with cavalry, especially with light cavalry. The history of every war is, or was until recently, the same. When it broke out, the authorities discovered that they had no light cavalry for reconnaissance and pursuit (whatever light cavalry there had been having

68

The height of masculine panache

become so cluttered with armaments as to have become heavy cavalry). They were, therefore, compelled to recruit auxiliaries, and these came in general from the less settled lands of eastern Europe. The first such recruits (employed by Louis XIV) were Hungarians and, in consequence, all hussars in all the armies of the world until the age of mechanization wore a fantastication of Hungarian national costume. Napoleon I employed Polish horsemen in a similar capacity, and, therefore, all lancers were put into Polish costume, with the characteristic square cap.

Cavalry uniform: Peace

All wars, especially long ones, affect military uniforms by jerking them back in the direction of utility; that is, the fighting dress of the soldier becomes less and less formal and more and more an approximation to the country or sporting clothes of the civilian. Wellington himself wore a dress which was hardly distinguishable from that of any private gentleman; General Picton fought the Battle of Waterloo in a civilian coat and a top-hat. In war-time clothes inevitably grow loose and 'sloppy', to the despair of sergeant-majors and military tailors.

Another factor is the need for light infantry, for reconnoitring and sharp-shooting, which always makes itself felt in war, although it is nearly always forgotten in times of peace. Light infantry are nearly always given some kind of protective colouring (it is amusing to find complaints in the early nineteenth century that this is 'unfair'), that is, jackets of green or dun colour with an absence of glittering accoutrements. Such uniforms have a certain modifying influence on those of the ordinary troops, so long as the war lasts.

Another curious thing that happens in war is the stereotyping of badges of rank. What has been merely a more gorgeous officer's coat with more embroidery on the sleeve becomes simply a coat with certain small insignia. It is interesting to note that by the middle of the Peninsular War a lieutenant-colonel had a crown on his straps and a major a star. Both wore two epaulettes; captains and subalterns wore only one (a very odd fashion), the former on the right shoulder, the latter on the left.

Cavalry uniform: War

War tends inevitably to make uniforms more utilitarian and less ornamental, but, the moment peace is restored, it is a very different story. In 1814, all the world was convinced that the long Napoleonic struggle was over, and Paris was full of

Allied troops. There were Cossacks in fur caps, loose blouses and wide trousers, there were Prussian grenadiers and Austrian whitecoats, there were hussars and cuirassiers and lancers; there were bearskins and plumed helmets and cockaded top-hats. The spectacle of foreign uniforms always excites the admiration of military tailors. Every national peculiarity of costume is noted, everything that tends to set off the military figure is admired, and the result is an attempt to adopt many details of foreign uniform.

Of all the headgear, none excited more interest and admiration than the square Polish caps of the various Lancer regiments. The French had adopted the Polish uniform for their *Chevaux-Légers* in 1811, and after Waterloo the British authorities did the same for three regiments of light dragoons. The Regent had a mania for well- (that is, tight-) fitting clothes, and when the new lancer uniform was being selected he ordered the commanding officer to attend at Carlton House to be fitted. The tailor was instructed to cut smooth every wrinkle and fine-draw every seam. The result was that a cavalryman was scarcely able to use his sword-arm.

When he became king in 1820 George IV revived the long-disused breast-plates for the Household Brigade, and gave the men helmets of bright steel with an enormous crest. In fact the helmet was so high that it could scarcely be kept on the head in a high wind, let alone in a charge. The bearskins of the Foot Guards were so much enlarged that taller sentry-boxes had to be installed round the Palace to accommodate them.

The chief result of all these improvements was to make military uniforms eminently unsuitable for war. 'Unfortunately,' lamented a reformer of the early '50s, 'we are too apt to adopt every novelty we see, regardless of utility. We have introduced the large-topped, over-weighted shako from the French; we have had the large trowser from the Cossack; the front of the coat padded and stuffed like the Russian. We have changed from one extreme to the other, without good reason; and we still have tight coats, stiff stocks, high caps and tall plumes, all of which it is to be hoped, for the comfort of our soldiers and the efficiency of our army, will shortly be got rid of.'

The leather stock was a particular absurdity. The soldier's neck was encircled with a band so stiff that he could not turn

70

Shooting costume, *c.* 1860

his head and could hardly bend it to look along the sights of his rifle. Yet men were sent to fight in this stock against the Indian mutineers. The same reformer demands most reasonably that the caps of both infantry and cavalry should be so designed that they would at least stay on the head in action; but even he was conservative enough to defend the scarlet coat as 'brilliant and imposing'.

The Crimean War—the first major European conflict since Waterloo—had the usual effect of making people realize that the uniforms of their soldiers were utterly unfitted to fight in. There was a general loosening up, the tunic finally replaced the tail coat, introducing, incidentally, a growing divergence between military and civil dress, although there was an obvious connection between the undress frock-coat of officers and the civilian mode of the day. Everything took on a slightly French look, for the French were very successful in the '50s and, after Magenta and Solferino, they imposed their military fashions on the world, as the successful nation always does. The American Civil War, to give an obvious example, was fought, both by North and South, in what were, in effect, *French* uniforms, even to the peculiar form of the *képi*.

Then in 1870 came the disaster of Sedan—and immediately the whole world went into German uniforms. The *Pickelhaube* had beaten the *képi* and some variety of the spiked helmet made its appearance in all the armies of the world. With very few exceptions the infantry regiments of this country adopted this spiked helmet, which remained in use, at first in battle and later for ceremonial occasions, until the First World War. But all the prestige of the German Army did not induce us to abandon our scarlet coats. It is true that rifle regiments (a quite obsolete term, for all British troops were by this time carrying rifles) wore green, but it was a green so dark as to be almost black and not at all inconspicuous in open country. The red coat even survived the disaster of Majuba Hill, and it was not until the Egyptian campaign of 1898 that khaki made its first appearance. The South African War which followed was a khaki war, and khaki has remained the fighting colour of British troops ever since.

Every war tends to drag uniforms back to the Utility Principle, but governments are sometimes slow to realize this and the early battles are fought in parade dress. The German

Battle dress suggested by a War Office committee, *c.* 1860

71

Modesty in Dress

Uhlans who reached the outskirts of Paris in 1914 were clad in the traditional 'Polish' costume, and the infantry wore the *Pickelhaube*. As this reflected the sun and revealed the position of the troops, it was at first (absurdly) covered with a detachable khaki cover before being abandoned for more practical headgear.

Sooner or later a 'battledress' has to be devised, and it is interesting to note that it is usually based on the popular sport of the time. A comparison between campaign clothes and civilian sports clothes shows that the Napoleonic Wars were fought, in effect, in hunting clothes, the wars of the second half of the nineteenth century in shooting costume, World War I in golfing costume. The British Government in 1939 had, for once, the sense to provide a battledress, resembling the clothes of a Canadian lumber jack, at the very outset of the campaign.

The uniform which has been discarded for active service then becomes 'walking-out dress', i.e. a smartened and tightened version of the battledress of the previous war. Ceremonial uniform is often the battledress of the last war but one. In the days of huge conscript armies this is only retained by the Household Troops, i.e. the ruler's bodyguard.

Modern uniforms are vestigial in two senses of the term. They have become on the one hand a parade, or walking-out, dress, and on the other have shrunk to mere insignia of rank or to miniature badges of territorial or regimental loyalty—a button and a pip. Before an actual assault even these are discarded. In modern warfare, therefore, the Utility Principle has triumphed completely, and the dress of commandos and tank crews is no more a uniform in the proper sense of the term than are the dungarees of factory hands. It is probable, however, that military uniforms will continue to exist, paradoxically, as the costume of a soldier when he is not fighting.

The paradox is, indeed, fundamental, for the two objects of military uniform are, in the end, incompatible. The first object is to inspire *esprit de corps* and to give a certain pride in his appearance to every member of it. A uniform makes a man feel more of a man and, of course, he *seems* more of a man in the eyes of the opposite sex. It is a truism that it is easier to find recruits for a smart, or 'crack' regiment, for when off duty it is the Guardsman who gets the girls.

A smart uniform enhances a man's masculinity and it does

72

Towards the Utility Principle

(This page and page 74.)
British officer of the First World

this in various ways. It gives him a head-dress which exaggerates his height; it puts a stripe on his trousers to exaggerate his apparent length of leg; it gives him epaulettes to exaggerate the width of his shoulders. It is the very epitome of the Pride of Life.

It would almost seem as if military uniforms had a life of their own and grew into certain forms independent of the conscious desires of those who wear them. Thus every cap that is put on a soldier's head tends to grow taller. The Guards' bearskin is an obvious case in point, for it was originally a soft cap (rather like a night-cap) with a narrow edge of fur. It was worn in the late seventeenth century by grenadiers who found it difficult to throw their grenades while wearing a three-cornered hat. Then the cap stiffened itself into the mitre-head-dress of the grenadiers we see in Hogarth's 'March to Finchley'. It was almost as if it had had an erection. Then the fur edge began to grow—and grow, until it swallowed the cap, a vestige of which can still sometimes be seen in a meaningless flap of cloth at the side of the large fur structure the headgear has now become.

The soldier wearing a bearskin (or any heavy and elaborate head-dress) is compelled to hold his head up, and this gives the feeling and the appearance of martial pride; and it is interesting to note that in the Guards Regiments the same effect is produced, even when the ceremonial bearskin is not worn, by giving the soldier a peaked cap which comes so low over his eyes that he is compelled to hold up his head to see in front of him.

But for a man to have '*tenue*' (which is, perhaps, a more precise word than 'bearing') he must not only hold up his head, he must constrict his throat. Hence the tight collars which always appear in military dress in a period of peace.

But towering head-gear and constricted throats are no use to men on the battlefield, and both have to be discarded. This is another example of the inevitable tug of war between parade costume and battledress which runs through the whole history of military uniforms. On the one hand we have pride in appearance and on the other its opposite, reaching its final term in camouflage. Camouflage is the desire to be invisible—and Modesty can hardly go further than that.

Vicarious Ostentation

6 The first social theorist to devote his attention to the curious phenomenon of vicarious ostentation was Thorsten Veblen. It was, indeed, part of the general thesis so convincingly expanded in *The Theory of the Leisure Class*. According to this theory, many of our institutions and modes of thought have come down to us from what he calls the 'barbarian culture', especially in its higher stages; that is, at a period when the accumulation of goods has begun. The beginning of ownership coincides with the emergence of a leisure class.

In more primitive periods, the hunter makes a real contribution to the subsistence of the group. The women may practise spinning and weaving, the manufacture of household implements and the cultivation of cereals, but flesh food is brought in by the hunter and the more successful he is, the greater is his prestige. Later, this prestige begins to be valued for its own sake and the distinction grows between 'noble' pursuits and 'menial' tasks. This distinction has persisted into our own day, although it has become somewhat blurred since Veblen wrote.

It is 'noble' to hunt and it is 'noble' to make war, and Veblen suggests that property was originally the booty of a successful raid. Such booty was honorific, and the more that could be accumulated the greater the honour. And it was, of course, important not only to possess many trophies but to show that you possessed them. 'The motive that lies at the root of ownership is emulation . . . The possession of wealth confers honour; it is an invidious distinction.'

Gradually accumulated property replaces the trophies of predatory exploit, and 'possessions come to be valued not so much as evidence of successful foray but rather as evidence of the prepotence of the possessor of these goods over the individuals within the community'. Property becomes

The nineteenth-century servant.

75

Proposed battle dress for British Army, 1952, based on the uniform of the German Afrika Korps. (Radio Times Hulton Picture Library).

the conventional basis of esteem. . . . The possession of wealth, which was at the outset valued simply as an evidence of efficiency, becomes, in popular apprehension, itself a meritorious act. . . . By a further refinement, wealth acquired passively by transmission from ancestors or other antecedents presently becomes even more honorific than wealth acquired by the possessor's own efforts.

It is unnecessary to reproduce all the arguments put forward by Veblen in support of his thesis. It is sufficient to note the ways by which men seek to display their wealth and therefore enhance the honour and esteem in which they are held. Veblen coined the phrases 'conspicuous leisure' and 'conspicuous consumption' to represent the most obvious of these methods. The first involves the creation of a 'leisure class', the distinctive character of which is that no member of it performs any useful or productive task.

> A detailed examination [he says] of what passes in popular apprehension for elegant apparel will show that it is contrived at every point to convey the impression that the wearer does not habitually put forth any useful effort. . . . Much of the charm which invests the patent-leather shoe, the stainless linen, the lustrous cylindrical hat, and the walking stick, which so greatly enhance the native dignity of a gentleman, comes of their pointedly suggesting that the wearer cannot when so attired bear a hand in any employment that is directly and immediately of any human use.

Of course, Veblen is speaking of the gentleman of the late nineteenth century; but if we have abandoned the 'cylindrical hat' and the patent-leather shoes, we still display linen at wrist and throat to show that we do not engage in any kind of manual toil.

> The dress of women [Veblen continues] goes even farther than that of men in the way of demonstrating the wearer's abstinence from productive employment. The woman's shoe adds the so-called French heel to the evidence of enforced leisure afforded by its polish; because this high heel obviously makes any, even the simplest and most necessary, manual work extremely difficult. The like is true even in a higher degree of the skirt and the rest of the drapery which characterises women's dress. The substantial reason for our tenacious attachment to the skirt is just this: it is expensive and it hampers the wearer at every turn and incapacitates her for all useful exertion. The like is true of the feminine custom of wearing the hair excessively long.

76

Late seventeenth-century print showing Austrian valets in doublet and

He then goes on to attack the corset which he describes as 'substantially a mutilation, undergone for the purpose of lowering the subject's vitality and rendering her permanently and obviously unfit for work'. Sixty years later, this criticism is obviously out of date. Today, most women have abandoned, or modified, the corset, abandoned long skirts and cut off their hair. One of the few relics of the display of 'conspicuous leisure' still remaining is the excessively flimsy and unpractical silk, or artificial silk, stocking.

A high social position is also indicated by 'conspicuous consumption'. This too has changed since Veblen wrote. Nowadays a rich woman does not display her superiority by sumptuosity or rich materials but by being quicker to adopt the latest fashion. This too is a diminishing advantage, for the multitude of fashion magazines and the practice of selling '*toiles*' to chain-stores, especially in America, enables the comparatively poor woman to catch up very quickly. A cynical millionairess once remarked to the present writer that the only advantage she gained by going to one of the great Paris couture houses was 'a fortnight's start'. However, there is one method still left of showing the world that your husband has a *very* important position in 'the Corporation'—and that is by wearing a number of diamond bracelets. From these it is said to be possible, at a party, to distinguish the president's wife from the wife of the senior executive. This is the Hierarchical Principle *in excelsis*—like the gold rings round a naval officer's sleeve.

Since men, at the beginning of the nineteenth century, made what has been called 'the Great Renunciation', it has been difficult for them to display their wealth (as Raleigh or Buckingham did) on their own persons. They therefore transfer their 'conspicuous waste' to their wives and mistresses. And for a long period of human history they were able to transfer it to their servants.

Veblen maintains that women themselves (in so far as their husbands are rich) fall into this category, for 'according to the ideal scheme of the pecuniary culture, the lady of the house is the chief menial of the household'. Perhaps this is to go too far, but he is certainly justified in pointing out the 'marked similarity...between the apparel of women and that of domestic servants, especially liveried servants'. Both are devised to display the pecuniary strength of the master of the household.

The discarded clothes of the eighteenth century are worn not only by the nineteenth-century servant but also by functionaries like this Colonial Governor.

Servants' dress is a subject which has not yet begun to receive the attention due to so important and interesting a part of the general history of costume. It is apt to be dismissed in a few lines, or taken for granted and omitted altogether from the works of those who set out to tell us of the changes which have come over human habiliments in the last four or five hundred years. This is a pity, for the study of servants' dress could be used to throw some light on the laws which seem to govern all the clothes we wear.

In the earliest civilization of which detailed records have come down to us—the Egyptian—servants seem to have worn no clothes at all, or very few. In the wall paintings the female slaves who are tending the guests at a banquet are wearing a decorated girdle resting loosely on the hips. Male attendants are provided with a thin loin-cloth and sometimes not even that. The wearing of clothes at that epoch was itself a class-distinction.

In later times the principle of vicarious consumption leads to the servants of important people being clothed quite elaborately, certainly much more splendidly than people of a similar class who are engaged in earning their own living. They are wearing the gorgeous clothes which their master cannot wear himself. Very often they are wearing his *discarded* clothes, at least in the figurative sense.

This is the key to the understanding of servants' dress throughout the ages. *Servants wear the discarded clothes of their masters.* Now the wearing of discarded clothes implies a time-lag and this time-lag also is the essence of the matter. Servants' clothes are perpetually out of date even when they have long ceased to be discarded clothes in the literal sense, and are as new and smart as possible for each individual servant.

Towards the end of the Middle Ages the question is complicated by the rise of what we can recognize as uniforms. The servants—the retainers—of a great noble formed a quasi-military body dressed alike and bearing the insignia of their lord. Originally the word livery meant what we would call an 'issue' and included food as well as clothing; later, it came to mean the clothing only, issued free to the servants of the great. The king, as the greatest of the nobles, followed a similar practice, and military uniforms, as we know them, were originally simply the king's livery.

Modesty in Dress

It is in the seventeenth century that a distinction can first be clearly traced between (military) uniforms and (civil) liveries. We find Louis XIV served by pages, sometimes of noble birth, who are wearing a livery, distinctly different from the clothes worn by the courtiers and by the King himself. This livery shows the time-lag already referred to very plainly, for below the more or less contemporary doublets can be seen the trunk hose of a previous generation. As the eye travels upwards over their costume we find that they grow more and more contemporary. Their neck-wear, for example, is similar to the King's own; and this too we find to be a fairly constant feature in servants' dress. It is not invariably so, however; for in the early eighteenth century we find servants wearing the falling collar of the previous century.

In the later eighteenth century servants' dress almost caught up with the contemporary mode, but when the great break of the French Revolution came we find that ordinary dress went on evolving, while servants' dress stopped short, as it were, at the barrier, and remained fixed for nearly a hundred years.

The footman's costume of the first half of the nineteenth century is the supreme example of the principles we have been discussing. The nineteenth-century footman wears the discarded clothes of the eighteenth century: buckled shoes, white silk stockings, knee-breeches, embroidered coat—even powdered hair. The coachman, of course, was even more atavistic in his attire. In addition to the footman's outfit he kept the wig and the three-cornered hat. The footman abandoned the tricorne very early in the nineteenth century, or even at the end of the eighteenth, but for some years he wore a *bicorne*.

In the pages of *Punch*, that invaluable seismograph of social change, we are able to trace the evolution of the footman from the early '40s until the present century. In 1842 we find him with frilled shirt, powdered hair, side-whiskers (almost, if not quite, meeting under the chin), epaulettes, and a huge bicorne, worn sideways on the head like Napoleon, but much bigger.

The bicorne seems to have gone out at the end of the '40s. The typical footman of 1850 has a top-hat with a gold-lace band and a cockade; and this cockade is such an extraordinary relic of the past that perhaps it is worth enlarging upon. The subject was first dealt with by that pioneer of the study of costume,

Dion Clayton Calthorp[1], who pointed out that the cockade was ultimately derived from the 'chaperon', a form of head-dress in fashion at the end of the fourteenth century. The chaperon was itself a stylized form of the medieval hood with its long tail, or liripipe, and dagged edge. It became the fashion to put the head instead of the face into the opening, to twist the surplus cloth round and to keep it in place with the liripipe. The chaperon is a 'made-up' head-dress of this kind. In the lord's colours it was frequently worn by retainers on the shoulder, and in that position dwindled to a mere device. Later, forgetting that it had been a hat itself, it became the *decoration* of a hat. It has been contended that the cockade should be confined to the servants of Royalty, but there is apparently no rule in the matter and certainly throughout the nineteenth century it was worn by almost every footman in private as well as official employment.

It is time, however, to return to a consideration of the other features of a footman's costume. In 1856 we find that 'Mr John Thomas of Belgravia' has abandoned not only his bicorne but his lace ruffles. He has a white tie and a stiff collar. He has all-the-way-round whiskers with shaved lips, and sometimes (we gather from the jokes in *Punch*) he is compelled to supply the deficiencies of Nature by wearing false calves. His hair is powdered white but his whiskers are either left their natural dark colour or even dyed black.

The footman had plenty to do in the ordinary upper-middle-class household. Larger establishments kept two or four footmen in addition to a butler, a coachman, a page and all the female servants. The single-handed footman had to wait at table, ride behind the carriage, and accompany the ladies of the household when they went shopping. In the '60s and '70s there were so many footmen waiting for their mistresses outside the early departmental stores that kindly managements provided benches in the doorway for them to sit on. It goes without saying that no young lady with any claims to gentility ever ventured into the streets alone. When the footman accompanied her he walked respectfully half a dozen paces in the rear. Except in summer, his outdoor uniform was a very long fawn-coloured overcoat with the inevitable top-hat.

It was in the middle of the 1870s that an entirely new style

[1] In an article in *The Sketch*, 9 March 1898.

of footman's livery made its appearance. Instead of the knee breeches trousers were worn, and instead of the laced coat there was a cut-away like the evening dress of the period, but plentifully sewn with metal buttons on the front and on the tails. The hair was no longer powdered but the side-whiskers were retained, although their size was much diminished.

It is interesting to note that once more a discarded garment had come into use as servants' costume. The tailcoat with the square cut-away ceased to be fashionable as day wear in the late '40s and early '50s. Most footmen were wearing it by 1880, that is, just a generation later. Of course, the old-style footman still persisted, but only in very grand houses, or in those whose owners, like *Punch*'s Sir Gorgius Midas, wished to appear very grand. A fashion plate of 1879 shows both types very clearly.

The waiter, however, is still with us; but being, as it were, a 'public' rather than a private servant, he is not of much use as a symbol of vicarious ostentation. Waiters in public restaurants in the early nineteenth century wore clothes which were more or less contemporary, but they went on wearing them when the diners had given them up. They also retained the mutton-chop whiskers which, in the last quarter of the century, had vanished from the faces of the clientele. If a film producer today wished to transform a restaurant into its aspect of a hundred years ago, all he would have to do would be to ask the customers to leave and the waiters to sit down at the tables. Until the First World War, diners in public restaurants (except in the grill room) were required to wear evening dress, but the dinner jacket was increasingly common and it almost seemed for a time as if the evening tailcoat would ultimately become 'waiters' uniform' and nothing else.

Within recent years, however, waiters themselves have changed. They have taken a hint from the dress of the ship steward, itself derived from the tropical kit of naval officers, and many waiters nowadays are clad not in more or less dingy black coats but in smart white jackets. The rest of the traditional costume is, in general, retained.

In France, however, the waiter usually wore an apron, and this custom still persists. Indeed the length of the apron (sometimes it is extremely long) is rigidly prescribed, and from this, and other minor variations, the knowing can deduce the waiter's place in the hierarchy of the establishment. Otherwise the line of development is the same as in England.

The clothes of female servants have never offered much opportunity for vicarious display, but they long retained certain vestigial features. The cap, now so bitterly resented as a mark of servitude, was once worn by every respectable woman indoors. And even fine ladies in the eighteenth century wore aprons. Once again we find the time-lag in servants' costume, but apart from such accessories, waitresses and chambermaids simply wore a sober version of the fashionable clothes of their own day.

Page boys' costume is simply (with all its buttons) a fossilized version of the dress of almost any boy in the 1830s. It is no longer seen in private houses but is still retained in the more pretentious hotels. This is in line with the general tendency for display to move from the private to the public sector. A man now shows what Veblen would have called his 'pecuniary strength' not by the magnificence of his own house but by the kind of hotel or restaurant he can afford to patronize. But it is still Vicarious Ostentation.

Footmen's liveries, *c*. 1900.

The Immodest
of Disguis

We think of a 'fancy-dress ball' (if anybody does think of such a thing in the modern world) as distinct from a theatrical performance. In the one, people dress up to amuse themselves; in the other, professional actors and actresses dress up to amuse an audience. But this distinction is a comparatively modern one; for the greater part of the long history of 'disguises' the two strands are inextricably intertwined.

In primitive times the whole tribe was involved in 'dressing up to dance', and if some of them (the women and children for example) did not actually perform, they were no mere audience. They were engaged in the same magical or religious ceremony: they were participants, 'communicants' one might almost say, not mere spectators. The history of the theatre is the widening gulf between those who act and those who watch until with the advent of the cinema, they may be six thousand miles and several years away.

Mid-eighteenth-century Ven
masquers by Pietro Longhi (M
Collection).

But if the theatre is ultimately derived from a primitive fertility dance, in developing along its own lines it left something out, and that something in the course of its history has been given different names: Saturnalia, Feast of Fools, Carnival—and fancy-dress ball. In such a progression it is evident that the religious element is less and less marked. What remains constant is the underlying eroticism which is itself transformed from a serious quasi-magical purpose to mere titillation. Yet it is strange how some of the most primitive features have persisted, and the three most striking of these are transvestitism, the use of animal masks, and the tendency to near-nudity.

The Roman Saturnalia took place on 17 December and was supposed to represent a return to the Golden Age of Saturn. To mark this, senators and knights laid aside the toga, slaves

84

were entertained at a banquet at which they were served by their masters, and the populace was allowed a degree of licence which would not have been tolerated at any other time of year. There was no punishment of criminals between 17 and 23 December; law courts and schools were closed and all work stopped.

The same reversal of the social conventions and the ordinary rules of behaviour was to be seen in the medieval Feast of Fools on New Year's Eve. When the verse in the Magnificat was reached, 'He hath put down the mighty from their seat, and hath exalted the humble and meek', it was interpreted in the most literal manner. The inferior clergy exchanged places and probably vestments with the canons, sitting in their stalls, censing the altar with black puddings and sausages, performing a burlesque of the Mass, and chanting a drinking song as they marched out of the church. Various efforts were made to suppress the Feast of Fools, but it long persisted. As late as 1445 the Theological Faculty of the University of Paris thought it necessary to issue a letter to the bishops calling upon them to put down 'an execrable custom permitted in certain churches, by which the Feast of the Circumcision is defiled. . . . Priests and clerks may be seen wearing masks and monstrous visages at the hours of office. They dance in the choir dressed as women, panders and minstrels.'

These may be thought of as the amusements of the people, but in the royal Courts the same spirit prevailed from time to time, and one such occasion obtained such celebrity, owing to its tragic ending, that it has been known ever since as the *Bal des Ardents*. The half-mad King of France, Charles VI, decided to celebrate the wedding of one of his wife's ladies-in-waiting with a ball at the now vanished Hôtel de Saint Pol in the east end of Paris. At the suggestion of Hugonin de Guisay, the organizer of most of the Court amusements, he decided that he and five of his boon-companions should be dressed as savages. Close-fitting suits of linen were steeped in a sticky resin and covered with loose flax resembling human hair. This was the accepted aspect of savages or 'men of the woods'. After the formal dancing, the King and his five friends slipped away and changed into this costume. Then they burst into the hall and pursued the ladies with demoniac shrieks. Suddenly a spark from one of the torches fell upon the nearest satyr and

85

R.Gaywood fecit

2.

Now Phœbus crownes our Sumer dayes   Summer   Her louely neck and brest are bare
With stronger heate and brighter rayes   Whilst her fann doth coole the Ayre

The modesty of the ve

R.Gaywood fecit

4

The cold, not cruelty makes her weare   For a smoother skinn at night
In Winter, furrs and Wild beasts haire Winter Embraceth her with more delight
                                                                    26577.4

and the modesty of the mask (etchings by R. Gaywood after W. Hollar, *c.* 1650).

in an instant he was ablaze from top to toe. The inflammable costumes of the others caught the flame. The King, who had been somewhat apart from the others, was saved, but two of the revellers perished on the spot, two more died soon after and another was so disfigured that he became a hermit. The King relapsed into complete insanity. The short escape from etiquette and decorum into a more primitive world had been dearly purchased.

During the Renaissance period, nearly all princely entertainments included some kind of fancy-dress ball. In general the costumes worn were Roman, for the attempt to revive the ancient world was what the Renaissance was about. But turbaned Turks were already beginning to make their appearance and the medieval 'wild men of the woods' were now denominated 'Americans'. Nymphs in diaphanous draperies and sometimes with bare breasts were a constant feature.

Such entertainments were for princely Courts, but the carnival provided, in Catholic countries, an opportunity for everyone to dress up in fantastic and sometimes lascivious costumes. The Roman carnival began eleven days before Ash Wednesday, but Friday and Sunday were excepted, so that there were eight days of gaiety. It was centred on the Corso and the Piazza Navona, used not for the first time for public spectacles, for it was built on the site of the circus of Domitian. For the greater part of the year it served as a market to which every visitor to Rome resorted. John Evelyn tells us that he spent an afternoon there inspecting the stalls of medals and antiques. Tournaments were held there, and tilting at the ring and, during August, the *piazza* was flooded on Saturday evenings so that water pageants could be staged. There were horse races, and foot-races in which naked Jews were compelled to take part until the Pope abolished the custom in 1688. Half a century earlier we learn from a contemporary *aviso*, of a 'palio of naked hunchbacks, very remarkable for the varied appearance of the malformation of their spines'.

All day and all night the Corso was crowded with masked figures wearing fantastic costumes and considerable licence prevailed in spite of the efforts of some of the popes to put a stop to it. They were not always supported by the cardinals. When Cardinal Albrizzi, in the act of serenading Queen Christina from a decorated car, heard the bell of the Gesù tolling for the forty hours (the signal that the carnival was over), he simply sent a message to the church ordering that the bell be stopped. Another Cardinal, however, Antonio Barberini, had the kindly idea of collecting the prostitutes in his coach (prostitutes were forbidden to ride in coaches), taking them round the churches and hearing their confessions.

In Naples it was the same story, for the Spanish viceroys positively encouraged the excesses of the carnival, which certainly served to distract the poor from the miseries of their daily life. The famous Duca d'Ossuna, who was viceroy from 1616 to 1620, provided public banquets for as many as ten thousand people; and in the carnival of 1617 ordered six carts to be prepared, each drawn by six horses. On each cart was a barrel of wine, a calf, fowls, hams, sausages and other eatables. The Viceroy appeared as a Turk in a turban and was followed by two hundred knights in grotesque costumes. At a given signal the mob surged forward and fought for the eatables on the carts.

Milan also was under Spanish rule and similar conditions prevailed, in spite of the efforts of St Carlo Borromeo, who complained that the most holy days of the year were profaned with tourneys and masquerades, and prohibited priests from taking part in them. He tried to prevent anything of the kind taking place near a church (where was often the most suitable open space) but he was not supported by the Governor, who organized a grand hunt outside the Cathedral itself. He was, however, compelled to transfer it to the square of the Castle.

The atmosphere of Florence was more staid and serious. It is true that the citizens were passionately addicted to the horse races run along the right bank of the Arno on the feast of St John the Baptist, but the ceremonies which accompanied the celebration of the saint were still of a purely religious character. The foreign dynasty—for Florence was ruled after 1737 by a Grand Duke of the Austro-Lorrainese House—thought to make itself still more popular by authorizing masquerades from the vigil of St John (23 June) until the evening of St Peter and St Paul (29 June), but the respectable Florentines (unlike their contemporaries in all the other states of Italy) refused to take part in them. The masks seen in the streets concealed the faces of the lowest dregs of the populace—and the police.

It was in Venice that, in the seventeenth and eighteenth

89

centuries, the carnival found its most extravagant expression. It began at Vespers on Twelfth Night and lasted until Lent, but there was also the festival known as the *Sensa*, 'a kind of summer aftermath of the carnival', at Ascensiontide, when the Doge set out in the Bucentaur for his marriage with the sea. All foreign visitors tried to arrive in time for the *Sensa*, including John Evelyn, who describes the crowd of gondolas on the Canalozzo, 'where the noblesse takes the air, as in our Hyde Park'.

The Piazza was crowded half the year with people in fancy dress and the scene is pictured for us by Molmenti, the social historian of Venice.

> It is a continual coming and going, a procession, an ant-heap of masked figures, a noise that is deafening . . . A harlequin murmurs sweet nothings into the ear of a young woman in a domino who laughs and takes refuge among the crowds. A *mattacino*, in white with red garters and red shoes, throws egg-shells filled with rose-water at patricians' windows. When night falls lanterns twisted with flowers are hung at the doors of the houses. Within there is feasting to the sound of pipe and viol. Everyone wears a mask. Old and young, patricians and plebeians, rich and poor, are all disguised.

One of Goldoni's characters calls the mask 'the finest convenience in the world': convenient, that is, for intrigue; and we can well believe that 'the women, made full use of the freedom which the mask gives them.'

The dialect poet Busenello compares the costumes to Ovid's *Metamorphoses*. 'A porter appears as a cavalier, a gentleman as a baker; a lady goes as her maid, the maid as her mistress, while a countess dresses like a country girl. There is no lack of fun on the Piazza after the Ave Maria.' Alas! the French invasion put an end to Venice as a political entity and the *Carnaval de Venise* was never the same after.

In Protestant England there was no carnival, but its place was taken to some extent in the eighteenth century by the pleasure gardens of Vauxhall and Ranelagh, enjoyed by all ranks of society except the very poor. Even Doctor Johnson confessed that 'when I first entered Ranelagh, it gave an expansion and gay sensation to my mind, such as I never experienced anywhere else'. Here, to celebrate the Peace of Aix-la-Chapelle in 1748, was held a 'jubilee-masquerade in the

Venetian manner', although there was only one gondola on a very small canal. Nonetheless Horace Walpole called it 'by far the prettiest and best understood spectacle I ever saw'; and he describes 'the whole garden filled with masks and spread with tents. . . . In one quarter was a Maypole dressed with garlands and people round it dancing to a tabor and pipe and rustic music, all masked, as were all the various bands of music that were disposed in different parts of the garden.'

A fortnight later there was another masquerade which the King himself attended clad 'in an old-fashioned English habit'. Various members of the nobility wore historical or quasi-historical costumes; but the sensation of the day was provided by the notorious Elizabeth Chudleigh, who appeared as Iphigenia, 'so naked that you would have taken her for Andromeda'.

There was such a dramatic change in women's costume in the last decade of the eighteenth century that the streets themselves might have been mistaken, by a visitor from a previous generation, as the scene of a fancy-dress ball. For all the women seemed to have discarded the formal attire of the *Ancien Régime* and to have adopted the dress of Ancient Greece with as near an approach to nudity as the law would allow—white muslin dresses were universal and sometimes so transparent that the pink tights could be seen underneath.

With the coming of the Romantic Movement in the early 1830s, there began a rage for what was imagined to be Tudor costume, with ruffs and puffed sleeves as if to indicate that the wearer was well versed in the novels of Sir Walter Scott. In the fancy-dress balls which were immensely popular at that time this element was even more marked, and with the growth of historical knowledge some of the attempts at 'period' costume began to be more or less 'correct'. With the Gothic Revival the imagination of Europe was suddenly filled anew with all the enchanted castles, moated granges, wandering knights and damsels in distress which had haunted the dreams of Don Quixote. Fancy-dress balls shared the impulse, but the medieval can never be a satisfactory setting for the masquerade, if only because it lacks the essential element of eroticism. One cannot even dance in plate armour, nor kiss on the stairs in a visored helmet. The upper classes, proud of their lineage, might like to see themselves as medieval knights, but most

91

people preferred easier and more seductive costumes when they dressed up to dance.

Under Louise-Philippe and Napoleon III there was an enormous number of dancing establishments in Paris and some of them, such as the Bal Bullier and the Mabille, retained their popularity for many years. They were much frequented by students and by their bitter enemies, the clerks and shop assistants, and, of course, by the women of the town. Some of the professional dancers and singers went on to triumph in the regular theatres. But the main purpose of the *bals* was, of course, dancing, and this was conducted in ordinary dress or in such an approach to evening dress as the patrons could afford.

Fancy dress seems to have been an exception, and certainly none of the *bals publics* could compete with the masked balls at the Opéra, then in the Rue Lepelletier, for the Second Empire had come to an end before Charles Garnier's Opéra was completed. Thanks to the lithographs of Gavarni, we have a whole picture gallery of those who took part in the masquerade, in every kind of costume, and all masked. There could be no doubt that most of the participants came to the Opéra in the hope of amorous adventure and, indeed, those who witnessed the spectacle speak of a veritable fever of eroticism. Under the mask all women were beautiful, and Arsène Houssaye has described in one of his most eloquent pages the disappointment which sometimes ensued when the mask was removed.

Many of the women were dressed in masculine costume, the tight trousers setting off to advantage the rounded forms of the *petite femme*. Transvestitism was also to be seen in the professional 'quadrilles' which formed part of the entertainment, the men dressed as nursemaids and the women as *pompiers* or soldiers. Apart from some extravagant décolletages, there was not much nudity of the kind which was one of the attractions of the *Bal des Quatz-Arts* later in the century, when 'attractions' always included a tableau of naked girls.

At the *bals masqués* at the Opéra it was possible to meet men of all ranks of society, but women of the upper classes never appeared there. Yet they shared in the common passion for disguises, and fancy-dress balls were popular in the most aristocratic houses and even at Court. No doubt by modern

Fancy dress ball costume, *c.* 1870

standards there was nothing provocative about the costumes, but the great crinoline skirts were somewhat shortened for the occasion. The looped-up skirt of the Empeor's mistress, the Comtesse de Castiglione, held in place by a brooch in the shape of a heart, provoked the Empress Eugénie's famous *mot: 'Vous portez votre cœur bien bas, Madame.'* But in general the balls at the Tuileries were extremely formal and proper, with the ladies in fashionable evening dress and the men in Court costume with knee-breeches and black silk stockings. However, once a year, at carnival time, there was a fancy-dress ball which gave an opportunity for fantasy in costume. One of these, that of 1863, was long remembered for its 'Ballet of the Bees', danced by the most exalted *grandes dames,* and this was followed by a scene in which 'five Court ladies, representing the Five Conti-nents, supported, in attitudes carefully studied before the mirror, a luminous globe, with, at their feet, naiads and nymphs, harmoniously grouped'.[1] The chronicler adds, maliciously, that the satyrs were missing—but were perhaps waiting in the wings. Unfortunately, we have no picture of the naiads and nymphs: it is almost certain that they were all wearing crinolines.

The Empress Eugénie had a, perhaps unfortunate, penchant for dressing-up as Marie-Antoinette; for the ball of 1866 she was clad in an exact replica of the dress shown in the portrait by Madame Vigée-Lebrun. The Emperor, with rather more tact, refused to appear as Louis XVI and contented himself with the great cloak of a Venetian senator worn over his ordinary costume. Princess Metternich wore Greek robes—with a crinoline underneath; Mrs Mills (one would like to know more of Mrs Mills) came as Amphritite in a green gauze tunic, laced with silver and decorated with sea-shells. The Marquise de Gallifet, in what we are assured was a *'jupe courte de cachemire blanc,'* represented the Archangel Gabriel! Two young American ladies, Miss Slidell and Miss Torrens, ap-peared, rather oddly, as Rain and Diana and were both clothed in tiger skins. We can well believe that they *'attirent tous les regards'.*[2]

At Compiègne the etiquette of the Tuileries was somewhat relaxed, and if fancy-dress balls were not often held there,

---

[1] Henri d'Alméras. *La Vie Parisienne sous le Second Empire.* Paris, n.d.
[2] Henri d'Alméras. *op. cit.*

there was a rage for *tableaux vivants* with a preference for 'classical' subjects. In these some of the aristocratic ladies did not hesitate to appear in white tights and very little else. This was part of the general passion for amateur theatricals, for, says the witty chronicler Auguste Villemot, 'in this age every salon is a theatre, every screen a *coulisse*, every father-in-law a prompter. And then there are, in this social comedy, a thousand situations in which *l'amour* and *l'amour-propre* have their part to play.' One amateur comedienne, who had a magnificent head of hair, actually commissioned a play in which she could appear as Eve, veiled only by her long tresses.

Fancy-dress balls were so popular in the second half of the century that nearly all fashion magazines had one or two plates, generally at Christmas time, showing suitable fantastic costumes. Some of these were more modest versions of stage costumes and were in general without much taste or originality; and indeed there was something tasteless in the fancy-dress ball itself, with its mad mixture of all periods, harlequins, peasants and the like.

Efforts were made to remedy this as, for example, in the 'Kermesse' of 1911 in the garden of the Palais Royal in Paris, where all the sales ladies (real ladies, as the affair was for 'charity') were dressed *à la* Marie-Antoinette. Paul Poiret was even more determined that there should be no mixture of styles. When he staged his famous 'Thousand-and-Second Night' in 1911 at his beautiful showrooms in the Avenue d'Antin, he insisted that all the guests should wear authentic Persian dress. Guests found at the entrance a line of scrutineers, who scanned their costumes with a critical eye. Those who were not habited *à la perse* were given the alternative of going to an upper room and changing into a Persian dress provided for them or returning home. Poiret did not intend that his carefully thought out ensemble should be marred by a single discordant note.

The general effect was of a scene for *Schéhérazade* and it is plain, in spite of Poiret's protests, that much of the impulse to dress up in this way came from the Russian Ballet, which had so recently taken Paris by storm. But, of course, there was a deeper motive: what might be called the harem-complex of Western man—and Western woman. Poiret himself was dressed as a pasha, his wife and some of her friends as oda-

94

lisques. And he describes himself as pursuing his 'lascivious concubines' with a whip. The 'Thousand-and-Second Night' must have been almost the last of such entertainments. World War I put an end to them and they have never been revived in anything like their old splendour. In the modern world the fancy-dress ball is as obsolete as the tourney.

AT THE BAL DE L'OPÉRA: A SAVAGE "GOMMEUSE."

The Exploitatio
of Immodest

8 If we accept the theory of the Shifting Erogenous Zone we must admit that nearly all *women's* clothes are an exploitation of immodesty. The theory is usually associated with the name of Professor J. C. Flügel who expounded it in his book *The Psychology of Clothes*. But before his time, other psychologists, even some pre-Freudian ones, had begun to explore this territory. However, for savants like Charcot, *zones hystérogènes* meant those parts of the body which showed symptoms of hyperaesthesia. It was Havelock Ellis who, in 1903, first used the term 'erogenous zones' in English. Two years later Freud adopted the doctrine not only on a pathological basis but as part of the normal process of sexual development. But he and later specialists were still concerned with the sensations of the epidermis: with the sense of touch.

Egyptian dancing girl.

It is plain that while certain garments (furs, for example) are capable of erotic stimulation to the wearer, before we can evolve any theory of the significance of erogenous zones to Fashion, we must stop thinking in terms of tactile sensations and transfer our attention to the sense of sight. In spite of Havelock Ellis's remark that 'It is undesirable, as well as inconvenient, to apply to a higher sense-organ a term which was devised for the special conditions of a more primitive sense-organ', this is what has happened. It is the effect of clothes on a spectator with which we are here concerned, and it was Flügel who made it possible to study it in a scientific manner. The present writer has endeavoured to push Flügel's theories further, and perhaps he may be permitted to reproduce the passage in which, in 1937, he tried to sum up his conclusions.

Dancing figures from an Italia
figure vase (Antiquarium, Berli

> Even those who still hold that clothing had its origin in modesty are as convinced as their opponents of the sexual significance of bodily coverings of all kinds. . . . The sexuality of the female body

96

is more diffused than that of the male and, as it is habitually covered up, the exposure of any one part of it focuses the erotic attention, conscious or unconscious, and makes for seductiveness. Fashion really begins with the discovery in the fourteenth century that clothes could be used as a compromise between exhibitionism and modesty. The aim of fashion ever since has been the exposure of, or the emphasis upon, the various portions of the female body taken in series.

The main fact that emerges from the experience of nudists in modern times is that while the imaginative contemplation of the naked body may be a highly erotic proceeding, the actual experience is exactly the reverse. It is not a matter of beauty or ugliness, but simply that the eye becomes so accustomed to the naked human body that this ceases to have any meaning to the imagination at all. Since the relaxations of prudery during the last twenty years or so, even the costumes of the lighter stage have exhibited the same law; in fact, men have become so used to seeing certain parts of the female body exposed that they no longer get any excitement out of the spectacle at all. In 1900 old gentlemen used to faint with emotion when they caught a passing glimpse of a female ankle. The modern young man can contemplate without emotion the entire area of the female leg and a considerable portion of the female stomach. In the 1920s for the first time for many hundreds of years, the female leg was exposed to general view . . .

In short, the female body consists of a series of sterilised zones, which are those exposed by the fashion which is just going out, and an erogenous zone, which will be the point of interest for the fashion which is just coming in. This erogenous zone is always shifting and it is the business of fashion to pursue it, without ever actually catching it up. It is obvious that if you really catch it up you are immediately arrested for indecent exposure. If you almost catch it up you are celebrated as a leader of fashion. The fashion that is coming in is always rather daring, the fashion which is going out is always rather dowdy, that is, it has exhausted its accumulation of erotic capital.

But the discussion of the exact way in which this mechanism operates must be left to a later chapter.

But if there is a sense in which all Fashion is the exploitation of immodesty, there is a further stage when some special occasion—a carnival, a pageant, a theatrical presentation—is used as an excuse for a degree of erotic appeal which would not be tolerated in ordinary life. In very primitive times erotic appeal was established by *putting on* clothes but, as soon as it became

97

the general custom habitually to cover the greater part of the female body, the removal of certain parts of the costume could be used as a sexual stimulant. And the more or less naked dancing girl has a very long history. She is seen on Egyptian wall paintings; she pirouettes round the circumference of Greek vases, she is depicted in the frescoes of Indian temples, she is cut deep into the façades of Angkor and Bangkok. If we define what we nowadays call a chorus girl as any young woman who combines a variable amount of dancing with a fairly constant amount of erotic appeal, she has a long history indeed. Even the cabaret, which we are apt to think of as a late off-shoot of theatrical entertainment, is an institution which has flourished, with some long intervals, from very early times. Indeed, the chorus girl may be said to have made her appearance in cabaret long before she appeared on the stage, and when we go to what Americans call a 'nitery' we are merely reverting to the habits of the pharaohs of Egypt, the wealthy Athenians, the Roman patricians and the caliphs of Baghdad, who all, however much they may have differed in other respects, seem to have enjoyed watching dancing girls performing before them as they reclined at their banquets.

In ancient Egypt we find dancing girls not only in the temples of the gods but in the houses of wealthy citizens of whose harem they formed a recognized part. No feast was complete without them. Like the other female servants, they wore nothing but a girdle resting on the hips and such bead collars and necklaces as their master chose to adorn them with. A typical feast of the Eighteenth Dynasty is depicted in a Theban tomb painting. 'The girls [says Adolf Erman in his *Life in Ancient Egypt*], wearing nothing but girdles, stand close to the wreathed wine-jars; they go through their twists and turns, clapping their hands to keep in time, meanwhile one woman plays the flute, and three others sing a song.' It is interesting to note that the song was a religious one and that alternate guests were priests.

In ancient Greece and Rome this connection with religion gradually became more tenuous. No feast was complete without what we should call a cabaret, but the performers were usually slave girls hired out for the occasion and handed over, when their performance was finished, to whichever of the guests happened to have taken a fancy to them. Thousands of

98

Masque costumes by Inigo
(Devonshire Collection, Chatsw
Reproduced by permission of
Trustees of the Chatsworth Settlen

years had to elapse before the profession became, in any sense, a respectable one, even when the slur of slavery was removed. Such performances were naturally frowned upon when Christianity became the dominant religion; but the dancing girl did not become entirely extinct, and one of them, under the reign of Justinian, was so successful that she actually married the Emperor himself. No other dancing girl in history has flown quite so high as the Empress Theodora, although many in more recent times have 'married into the peerage'.

The Dark Ages which followed the collapse of the Roman Empire were dark indeed. But when the records begin again we find representations, sometimes in the margins of illuminated manuscripts, of the entertainers who beguiled the tedium of the medieval baronial hall. For the most part there were men plucking harps and chanting interminable epics of military prowess, but there were also jugglers and tumblers among them, and some of these were women. By ancient or modern standards they were conspicuously overdressed.

Renaissance pageant car with *figurante*.

However, with the coming of the Renaissance the chorus girl in the form of the *figurante*, 'posing beauty', or showgirl (as she is called in a modern revue), makes a startling reappearance. When a royal or other important personage was about to make a state entrance into a town, it was the custom to mobilize some of the more beautiful girls (still, of course, of the non-respectable classes) and to group them around—or even in—the city fountain to represent water-nymphs. During the sixteenth century, with its passion for everything classical, this practice became increasingly popular until no royal visit could be said to be complete without it. At the wedding of Cosimo de' Medici and Eleanor of Toledo, which took place in Florence in 1539, nymphs and sirens, tritons, fauns, satyrs, and shepherds sang and danced; and when Francesco de' Medici married Joanna of Austria the bridal pair was attended by Venus and the Graces.

Queen Maria of Hungary, Stadholder of the Netherlands, offered such magnificent entertainments to her brother, the Emperor Charles V, and her sister, Queen Eleanor of France, that they became proverbial. At one of these a castle was stormed by a thousand men and defended by ladies dressed as nymphs—that is to say, in diaphanous draperies that displayed their legs and sometimes exposed their breasts. This undoubt-

99

edly accounted for a good deal of the enthusiasm for such performances.

There were 'nymphs' at the marriage of the future Henri IV to la Reine Margot in Paris; and on the occasion of the meeting between Charles IX and his sister the Queen of Spain, when the banquet had been cleared away, 'satyrs bore in a brightly lighted rock. Upon this rock perched nymphs whose beauty and magnificent jewels radiated an even greater brilliance than the artificial lights illuminating the rock.' In 1585 Francesco, Grand Duke of Tuscany, at the marriage of his sister to Cesare d'Este, arranged an elaborate series of festivities, of which we have a record, unfortunately without pictures. There are, however, full descriptions of the scenery and costumes, from which we learn that Beauty was represented by 'a most beautiful girl with blonde hair like gold thread, her breasts exposed, but modestly and with grace'. The costume of Venus, however, was '*lascivissimo*, as befitted the Mother of Love'. The Victoria and Albert Museum possesses engravings of the splendid pageants organized at Württemberg in 1609 and 1616, and these included festival cars occupied by nymphs whose costumes, or lack of them, anticipate those of the Folies Bergère. The fashion for such entertainments spread to England, and Chatsworth House still possesses drawings by Inigo Jones of the costumes of the participants; and in some of these the women are extravagantly décolletée, even to the exposure of the breasts.

The Court masques of Jacobean England were, of course, private entertainment, and ladies of the highest nobility did not hesitate to appear in them. Later in the century, at the Court of Louis XIV, when such entertainments had become more professional, we find the wife of Molière appearing as a *figurante* in one of the scenes of *Les Plaisirs de l'Île Enchanté*.

Until the end of the seventeenth century royal entertainment was a complex affair comprising a mock tournament, a royal procession, a play, a ballet, a banquet and firework display. In the early eighteenth century these elements fell apart, leaving opera and ballet as separate entities, the performers in both being professionals performing not for the amusement of courts but in public theatres. And opera almost always included a ballet which, before the elaboration of a special technique of ballet dancing, was not very different

'Poses plastiques', *c*. 1850.

Nineteenth-century chorus girl plaining to the manager of a theatre of the exiguity of her cost

from the dancing scenes in a revue. Then the female costume in the ordinary sense underwent a revolution, and by 1800 women in ordinary life were wearing diaphanous muslin dresses. Stage costume followed suit and it became necessary to adopt a *maillot* underneath. It is amusing to note that in the States of the Church such *maillots* were required to be blue, lest by any chance their close-fitting forms should be mistaken for naked flesh.

After the success of Taglioni in *La Sylphide*, ballet costume stereotyped itself into the famous *tutu* or white ballet skirt, which lasted until the end of the century even in ballets where the *figurantes* were clothed more or less correctly in fancy or period costume. The skirts of the *tutu* gradually became shorter and shorter until it resembled a powder puff and, in an age when the female leg was hardly seen at all in ordinary life, exercised a considerable erotic appeal.

The well-known miscellaneous writer Albert Smith published in 1847 his *Natural History of the Ballet Girl*, and he paints for us a vivid picture of the dancing girl of the period. After telling us that 'We intend to touch but lightly on pink tights and gauze petticoats', he goes on to describe the typical *tutu*, with its 'innumerable muslin petticoats excelling even the capes of a night cabman's coat in the number of their layers'.

Privileged persons were still allowed 'behind'. The stage-door johnnie of a later age was a poor survival, who had been turned out into the street instead of being allowed to wander at will in the wings. In 1847 the 'loungers in the *coulisses* soon began their flirtations with the *coryphées*'. Smith was astonished at the banality of their conversation, but that was not the point. This was the period when every man of fashion thought it necessary to 'protect' a ballet girl. And the girl who could not find such a protector had, with her fifteen shillings a week, a pretty hard life.

In the early 1880s pantomime—at least the big spectacular pantomimes at Drury Lane—began to exhibit some of the characteristics of what we should call revue. The troupes of *figurantes* or showgirls were swelled to prodigious proportions and their costumes were made as gorgeous and as exciting as the taste of the time allowed. William Pitcher, who, in order to assume the prestige of the foreigner, called himself Wilhelm, was the stage costume designer most in vogue; and we find

101

serious art magazines devoting articles to his designs, with the remark that 'Were it not for the delicate artistic instinct which made these exquisite displays a charming possibility, there would be little temptation to throw open our pages to the subject'. Wilhelm is praised as 'an artist of infinite resource, of rich and graceful invention, and yet possessed of that reticence in taste whose sense of refinement controls an imagination at once poetic and dainty, and whose colour sense is equally opulent and chaste'. Most of the designs he made, reproduced with the articles, are equally chaste except for one lady whose thighs might truly be described as opulent.

Wilhelm based his work upon that of the French artist Alfred Grévin, the inventor of the *petite femme* in the *Journal Amusant*. In this we find a number of back-stage scenes showing the *gommeux* (or swells) making up to the *figurantes*, and even one or two designs with girls complaining to the management about the exiguity of their costumes. Grévin himself designed costumes for the lighter stage and his work was considered of sufficient importance to be listed in Béraldi. His most famous costume was that for the 'Swallows' in a piece entitled *Le Voyage dans la Lune* produced at the Gaîté in Paris. This created a sensation and inaugurated a new world of fashion in theatrical costume.

The piece was brought to London in 1876 and presented at the Royal Alhambra Theatre, Leicester Square. It was described in the programme as a 'Grande Opera Bouffe in Four Acts and Fifteen Tableaux; music by Offenbach . . . dresses after designs by Mons. Grévin (of Paris)'. The dancers were French and the excitement they caused was due to the fact that they had (or appeared to have) naked thighs with suspenders stretched across them to keep up the stockings. So popular was this costume that it was frequently imitated, and in a drawing of the 'Swallow costume' in the author's possession, it is interesting to note that while, in the design, the thighs are clad in *pink* tights, there is a note on the back indicating second thoughts on the part of the management: 'Tights grey at top same shade as shoes—no flesh.' It is curious to note how this 'Naked-thigh-spanned-by-suspender' complex has persisted. In spite of modern revivers of the Can-Can it was not, however, characteristic of the dancers of the Moulin Rouge. A glance at the poster of Toulouse-Lautrec is enough to show that they wore quite long drawers. It was left to Marlene Dietrich to revive it with spectacular success in the film 'The Blue Angel'—but this time, as in modern revue, the thighs really were naked.

It was an artist named Comelli who, in the 1890s and the early years of the present century, was the great exploiter of the female thigh, covered of course with tights. The nudity we see is only apparent, but perhaps none the less provocative for all that. And what thighs they were! So completely has taste changed, so different now is our ideal of feminine beauty, that the show-ladies of the '90s appear to us almost as monstrosities. The hips, made to look even wider than they were by pinching in the waist and hanging the figure with horizontal draperies, assumed gigantic proportions. Fortunate, perhaps, that the owners of such hips were not expected to dance but only to walk in a stately manner from one side of the stage to the other.

A generation before, the whole female body clad in tights had frequently been exposed to public view in some of the night haunts of London. The *Swell's Night Guide through the Metropolis* (1841 edition) informed its readers of two 'Temples of Voluptuousness' in the Waterloo Place neighbourhood where girls, mostly French, 'in every possible state, from complete nudity to half dressed, go through the most voluptuous exhibitions—imitate the classic models and perform the most spirit-stirring dances'. The 'classic models' were, and long remained, a frequent excuse. *Tableaux vivants* were also to be seen in the 'Hall of Rome' at the Windmill Saloon, Windmill Street—a curious anticipation of the famous Windmill Theatre, established almost on the same spot, certainly in the same short street—in the early 1930s. The swell who wished for a night out in the 1840s could also attend the famous Judge and Jury Society established at the Garrick's Head Hotel in Bow Street by 'Baron' Nicholson. He later moved to more commodious premises, first at the Town Hotel opposite Covent Garden Theatre and later at the Coal Hole Tavern. The principal part of the entertainment consisted of a mock trial, a kind of parody of cases actually before the real court. Needless to say, they were all of the *crim. con.* variety. The 'Mimic Court of Law' was followed by *poses plastiques* of girls in pink tights, referred to by the 'Baron' as 'slightly-veiled daughters of Venus'. Similar performances were staged in the Provinces.

Modesty in Dress

For the *tableaux vivants* presented at the Parthenon Rooms, Liverpool, in 1850, the titles of the scenes, '*The Sultan's Favourite Returning from the Bath*' and '*Diana Preparing for the Chase*', tell their own story.

In France the passion for *tableaux vivants* spread not only among the *demi-monde* but even in high society and the Court itself. They were staged at Compiègne and were supervised by artists of the calibre of Cabanel and Viollet-le-Duc. *Grandes dames* did not hesitate to appear in mythological scenes and the *demi-mondaines* were even less reluctant to expose their charms. The Emperor's mistress, Marguerite Bellanger, appeared nude on the stage and recalls the fact proudly in her memoirs.

Many of the *poseuses* who appeared in London were, in fact, French, and English moralists liked to think that all such women had been 'imported from abroad'; and they were confirmed in this view by the introduction in Paris of the scandalous Can-Can. This did not involve nudity but it did involve a large display of underclothes which, to many spectators, seemed even more exciting.

The *danseuse* whose stage name was Finette (the mistress of Whistler and the subject of one of his finest etchings) was the first woman to dance the Can-Can in England, in a pantomime staged on Boxing Day 1867 at the Alhambra, Leicester Square. But she wore male costume on this occasion 'and, therefore, much of the objection which an English audience would have had to the French dance was removed'. Much of the interest, also, one would have thought. Two years later, however, a real Can-Can was danced by women in women's clothes at the St James's Theatre as the finale of Offenbach's *Orphée aux Enfers*. *The Times* stigmatized it as outrageous and advised all respectable persons to leave the theatre (presumably in a marked manner) before it took place.

Shortly afterwards a similar performance at the Alhambra was visited by two police officers who found little to complain about except that 'more of the thigh is visible in consequence of wearing very scanty drawers'. However, the Can-Can did get into the courts in consequence of a libel action brought by the manager of the St James's Theatre against the magazine *Vanity Fair*, whose theatre critic had condemned Offenbach's *Vert-vert* as 'introducing the worst orchestra, some of the flattest

104

An original design for a stage 'Swa

singing and one of the most indecent dances in London'. The defence called no less a person than the Lord Chamberlain, the Marquess of Hertford (a later Lord Hertford, of course, than Thackeray's wicked Lord Steyne) who said that the dance was neither graceful nor artistic but purposely indecent. A few days after the verdict, which was in favour of *Vanity Fair*, his Lordship issued a manifesto against the 'indecent dances and immodest dresses which now form so prominent a part of the entertainment at some theatres'. The result of all this was that the Can-Can was banished for a time, although Lottie Collins performed a somewhat Anglicized version of it after singing her famous song 'Ta-ra-ra-boom-de-ay'. In the 1890s there was an attempt to get the Lord Chamberlain to ban all performances by women in 'visible tights', or whose skirts were 'more than four inches above the ground, or whose bust was partly exposed, or whose skirts opened at the side', but this morality campaign came to nothing.

The rise of musical comedy, under the aegis of George Edwardes, introduced another type of chorus girl, or rather of 'chorus lady'. She was hardly ever required to wear fantastic or revealing costumes. In general she wore the fashionable dress of the day as an alleged guest at one of the innumerable garden parties or weekend visits which the writers of musical comedies thought it necessary to include in their plots. The 'Gaiety Girl' of tradition was, on the stage, simply a smart woman clad in the contemporary fashion.

Theatre-goers who are now middle-aged will remember the witty number in the revue *Streamline*, presented by C. B. Cochran at the Adelphi Theatre in 1934. The first scene of 'Eve-volution', as it was called, showed the chorus girl of fifty years ago, clothed from ears to ankles and contenting herself, as far as dancing was concerned, with twirling a provocative parasol. But behind the scenes, her life was a series of parties and assignations. By contrast, we were shown the modern chorus girl, wearing almost nothing on the revue stage, but no sooner off it than she hurried home to a cup of cocoa with mother.

Revue, as a recognized form of theatrical entertainment, began in a very humble way. It was originally a mere turn in a variety programme, and, in England at least, remained so until the outbreak of the First World War. In France, it kept

for a long time its original character of a witty commentary on
current events; and in the smaller theatres in Paris this element
still remains. The spectacular side, however, soon predomi-
nated, as theatrical managers realized that at last they had
discovered an elastic framework in which could be united all
those appeals to the eye which before had been scattered in
baller, pantomime, comic opera and musical comedy.

Even before the First World War some of the French theatres
were putting on shows with a considerable amount of nudity,
breasts and navels being freely exposed; and when Paris, during the war, became the city of pleasure for troops on leave,
the Allied soldiers were introduced to these delights. By contrast, the revues in London had comparatively little nudity,

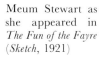

Costumes in *Sitting
Pretty*, a Paramount
film, 1934.

Meum Stewart as
she appeared in
The Fun of the Fayre
(*Sketch*, 1921)

such entertainments as *The Bing Boys on Broadway* being conspicuously overdressed by modern standards. There was one
scene in *Chu Chin Chow* in which the slave-girls were *supposed*
to be naked under an enveloping cloak but they turned their
backs to the audience before opening the cloak.

During and immediately after the war, revues in London
were popularly known as 'leg-shows'—a revealing phrase
which became meaningless in 1925 when the female leg was
lavishly displayed in ordinary dress. Soon revue costume settled down into a well-defined and recognizable type. Those

106

who take the trouble to look at photographs, even of the revues produced immediately after the First World War, will be astonished to realize how recent this type is, how very new is the costume which everybody now accepts as normal for the chorus girl. Tights and stockings were the first to go, skirts of any kind became exceptional and, in the middle 'twenties, a gap appeared between pants and brassière which, sometimes narrower and sometimes wider, seems now to have become a permanent feature of revue costume, but the navel was never exposed except by cabaret and 'speciality' dancers. In *Ever-Green*, staged by Cochran, one scene was supposed to represent a French music-hall (that is, with every excuse for nudity) but the gap at the midriff was filled in with gauze. It was not until the 1930s that stage costume in England really shed its inhibitions, but at first only in the most tentative way. In an alleged 'French' revue put on at the Victoria Palace in 1930, the nude figures were wax dummies.

At the Prince of Wales Theatre in 1934 a showgirl posed with naked breasts, but behind a gauze veil, and in two scenes the chorus danced with navels exposed on the first night. Later the management repented and provided little silver triangles to hide them. This was also done in a scene in Cochran's production of *Nymph Errant*. *West End Scandals*, presented at the Garrick Theatre in 1934, had two *figurantes* facing the audience and naked to the waist, but they were subsequently covered with a gauze veil.

It was only the little Windmill Theatre at this period which dared to put on a totally nude *figurante*, but she was seen sideways and well towards the back of the stage. Later, posing nudes became a commonplace at the Windmill and these were tolerated by the authorities *on condition that they did not move*.

The real breakthrough came after the Second World War when the would-be exploiters of immodesty suddenly had a revelation. For years serious plays which could not obtain a licence for public performance had been presented by 'theatre clubs'. By a curious quirk of English law these were immune from the Lord Chamberlain's jurisdiction. But if such *plays* could be so presented, why should not revue promoters claim a similar liberty on condition that the theatre became a club and the show was given 'for members only'? As membership could be obtained on application at the door, the distinction

107

between 'club' and public theatre was almost non-existent; but the device worked and the pioneer enterprise in Irving Street, off Leicester Square, was so successful that imitators sprang up all over London. Soon London outstripped Paris in nude spectaculars of all kinds, particularly that known as strip-tease.

It is true that something of the kind had long been known in America as part of what was known as Burlesque. It was a somewhat crude entertainment flourishing in the less fashionable quarters of New York but the Minskys and a few other enterprising impresarios promoted it to Broadway status, and for a time it had almost a fashionable vogue. The whole point of Burlesque was the exploitation of female nudity, the nude parades being interrupted, to give the girls time to change, by 'comic business' of almost unbelievable vulgarity.

The Burlesque managers seem to have stumbled on strip-tease almost by accident. At one of the clubs for 'tired business men', appeared a girl named Jacqueline Joyce who came on covered with furs and proceeded to shed them one by one. She explained that she was a Canadian and that her relatives were trappers; actually she was from the Southern States. She was a great success and the Minskys—or their press agent—had a brilliant idea. They 'grabbed a quarter of a million dollars' worth of publicity by complaining about her to the House Immigration Committee on the ground that stripping was an American art and no foreign competition should be allowed'.[1] Certainly there was no lack of talent at home with Gipsy Rose Lee being perhaps the best known from coast to coast. She started in the box-office of the Republic Theater, but, shedding her inhibitions, promoted herself to the stage—and to the top of the bill.

The strip-tease routine was so popular that some night-club proprietors decided to present nothing else, and two of them, Wilner and Callaghan, remodelled a private house on 52nd Street, a few doors from Fifth Avenue. The staircase had balustrades shaped like women's legs; the walls were decorated with pictures of famous nudes: Eve, Botticelli's Venus, Lady Godiva. The bar was a bedstead and it was intended that the bar-tenders should wear pyjamas and the girl cashier a night-dress.

Bal Tabarin, Paris, 1934.

[1] H. M. Alexander. *Strip Tease. The Vanished Art of Burlesque.* Knight. New York, 1938.

108

But the 'joint' never opened, for in April 1937 the blow fell on the whole world of Burlesque. A certain Mr Sumner of the Society for the Suppression of Vice served a complaint against the Gotham Theater, and the case was heard in the Court of Special Sessions, New York. Some of the witnesses amused the public so much that the judge felt constrained to say: 'If there are persons here for entertainment purposes, I'll ask them to step out.'

The stage electrician seemed to be the chief witness for the defence, and he was duly cross-examined by the district attorney. The vital question seemed to be whether he had ever seen a strip-woman 'working in a white light'. He said 'no', and all the witnesses were equally emphatic. The public expected an acquittal but, to everybody's surprise, the verdict went against the theatre.

The immediate result was a rush to all the Burlesque theatres, but it didn't last, for in a few days they were all put out of business. Burlesque shows were raided by the police and the girls packed off in police vans. The theatres were closed and the night clubs dropped the strip-tease. They were afraid of losing their liquor licences.

Meanwhile strip-tease had spread to England, to the alarm of the Public Morality Council. The Bishop of London wrote letters to the Press and promoters of strip-tease shows were prosecuted and fined. This was in 1939, and in the following year the Lord Chamberlain summoned a conference with the aim of banning all stage nudity. Then came the war and strip-tease for a while was forgotten.

It revived again in the 1950s, and by 1960 it was estimated that there were two hundred strip clubs in London and a hundred more in the provinces. Such clubs, as we have noticed, were supposed to be free from police interference, but some of them put on shows of such open indecency that the authorities felt that something had to be done about it. Some clubs were prosecuted and the proprietors heavily fined. Those that escaped continued to flourish and even to multiply, as can be seen today by anyone strolling through Soho. London indeed is supposed to be the Mecca of the strip-tease industry, surpassing America or any country on the continent of Europe. Paris would seem to have fallen far behind, at least so far as strip-tease clubs are concerned. There is a strip-tease act in

109

many Parisian revues, but, after all, there is something ridiculous in the spectacle of a girl solemnly taking off her clothes on a stage already crowded with naked women. At the time of writing, London is still leading in the exploitation of immodesty.

The cinema has always lagged a little behind the stage in the exploitation of immodesty. In its early days the subject-matter of films was either a simple form of documentary or was drawn from the world which Elmer Rice satirized as the country of 'puerilia'. Its heroines were the heroines of old-fashioned melodrama, blameless girls 'of rural origin . . . faced with the devastating alternatives of allowing [their] aged parents to be turned out of doors, or of giving [themselves] in marriage (or in many cases, to a state far less honourable than marriage)'[1] to wicked land-owning baronets threatening to 'foreclose on the mortgage'. The ideal interpreter of such girls was the young woman originally known as Dorothy Nicholson and then as—Mary Pickford.

The funny films, the Keystone comedies and early Chaplins, were equally moral. It was not until the middle '20s that the film-makers began to realize that the medium had other possibilities which can be summed up in one word—Sex. Motion pictures began to bear such titles as *The Daring Years*, *Sinners in Silk* and *The Price She Paid*. Film publicity promised such alluring themes as 'beautiful jazz babies, champagne battles, midnight revels, petting parties in the purple dawn . . . red kisses, pleasure-mad daughters, sensation-craving mothers . . . the truth—bold, naked, sensational'.[2]

It is true that very few of the actual pictures managed to live up—or down—to such promises; but the world's moral guardians, official or self-appointed, began to be alarmed. The Child Welfare Committee of the League of Nations met at Geneva in May 1926 to consider the 'Effect of the Cinematograph on the Mental and Moral Well-being of Children'. They came to no effective conclusion but shortly afterwards the film producers themselves began to think that they had better put their house in order. So Mr Will Hays, an elder of the Methodist Church, became president of the Motion Picture Producers and Distributors of America with the implied function of keeping the party clean.

Casino, London, 1936.

[1] Elmer Rice. *A Voyage to Puerilia*. 1930.
[2] Frederick Lewis Allen. *Only Yesterday*. 1931.

Great Britain showed a similarly oblique approach by extending the power of a local licensing authority 'to matters other than the safety of the audience', i.e. fire prevention, and so enabling it to 'assume the functions of a censor'. An unofficial body known as the British Board of Film Censors was set up and, among other activities, it drew up a list of scenes which might not be shown on the screen. These ranged from 'cruelty to young infants' to 'gruesome murders and strangulation scenes', and included 'indecorous dancing', 'improper bathing scenes', 'views of men and women in bed together', 'nude figures' and 'unnecessary exhibition of women's underclothing'. It must have been a puzzling task for the film censors to decide when the exhibition of women's underclothing was 'unnecessary'. In actual fact undressing scenes were frequently shown and had the curious effect of immensely improving women's underwear in real life: the abandonment of linen and the substitution of real or artificial silk.

Most of the prohibitions proved ineffective. The Czechoslovak film *Ecstasy*, produced in 1933, shows Hedy Lamarr bathing in a lake completely nude and then darting through the shrubbery, in the same state, when her solitude is invaded. However, it was many years before the film could be shown uncut in either England or America.

On the continent of Europe the authorities were more permissive. Abel Gance's *Lucrezia Borgia*, produced in France in 1935, contained an 'orgy' scene with semi-nude women, and *La Tour de Nesle* of 1937 showed some of the revellers with exposed breasts. The American censors were much concerned with décolletage of any kind and *Nell Gwynne* was banned because of the excessive 'cleavage' of Anna Neagle. It is amusing to note that, in England, 'poor Nelly' only got past the censor by being shown in a quite unhistorical scene as dying in poverty, as a punishment for her sins.

At the present day the moral atmosphere is much more permissive, even on the public screen, and if you call your little cinema a 'club' you can show almost anything. Indeed the 'man and woman in bed together', once so sternly forbidden, is now almost obligatory, and a dozen films have left no doubt in the public mind of the beauty of Martine Carol's breasts and Brigitte Bardot's whole body. The old prohibitions seem simply to have faded away.

Frou-Frou and Fetishisr

9 If the student looks up 'Fetishism' in the catalogues of most libraries he will find himself referred to the cult-objects of African tribes. This is in line with the anthropologists' use of the term, but the psychologists give the word another meaning. For Binet (followed by Lombroso, Krafft-Ebing and Havelock Ellis), fetishism or 'Erotic Fetishism' as they prefer to call it, means 'the tendency whereby sexual attraction is unduly exerted by some special part or peculiarity of the body or by some inanimate object which has become associated with it'. Havelock Ellis speaks also of 'a symbol which has parasitically rooted itself on the fruitful site of sexual emotion and absorbed to itself the energy which normally goes into the channel of healthy human love. . . . The lover's attention is diverted from the central focus of sexual attraction to some object or process which is on the periphery of that focus, or even outside of it altogether, so recalling it by association of contiguity or of similarity.'

In this sense one might say that clothes themselves are a function of fetishism and that it is only on this basis that Flügel's theory of the 'shifting erogenous zone' can be properly understood, but in this chapter we shall confine ourselves to the more usual and restricted use of the term. The field is still wide enough for, as Stanley Hall remarks, 'there is almost no feature, article of dress, act, that may not have to some morbid soul specialized erogenic or erethic power'.

It has been contended that some degree of fetishism is present in all but the grossest forms of sexual desire, and we find so 'advanced' a woman as Mary Wollstonecraft declaring that 'devotion and love may be allowed to hallow the garments as well as the person, for the lover must want fancy who has not a sort of sacred respect for the glove or slipper of his mistress'.

The glove or slipper! Havelock Ellis tells us that glove-

112

Polaire, *c*. 1908.

The extreme of tight-lacing.

fetishism is rare but that shoe-fetishism is extremely common; in fact he claims that it is the most common of all and that 'even for the normal lover the foot is one of the most attractive parts of the body'.

Until recent times this was certainly the opinion of the Chinese, especially in the south of China. Dr J. Matignon tells us that 'when a Celestial takes into his hand a woman's foot, especially if it is very small, the effect upon him is precisely the same as is provoked in a European by the palpation of a young and firm bosom'. In European eyes it seems even stranger that the voluptuous sensation is actually increased when the foot is mutilated by having been tightly bound up in childhood, and there is surely a parallel here with the excessive tight-lacing of European women which persisted almost until our own day. But this theme must await further development later.

Particularly small feet, as well as small hands, are, as Veblen has pointed out, a sign that the owner of these attributes is not accustomed to work. They are therefore a symbol of 'conspicuous leisure' with all the social prestige that it implies. But the Hierarchical Principle alone would not be sufficient to explain the passion with which small feet have sometimes been regarded.

The ancient historian Strabo tells the story of a certain courtesan named Rhodope whose sandal was carried off by an eagle and dropped in the lap of the King of Egypt while he was administering justice. The King could not rest until he had discovered to whom this delicately small sandal belonged; he sought her out and finally made her his Queen. This might be regarded as the prototype of Cinderella and the little glass slipper. It was not until prostitutes were compelled by law to wear sandals or slippers that the closed shoe was reserved for respectable matrons, who took every precaution not to display their feet.

113

An echo of this idea persisted for many centuries in Spain where, as late as the seventeenth century, laws were passed to forbid the feet in paintings of the Virgin to be shown naked. The father-in-law of Velazquez, himself a painter, after remarking on these prohibitions, cried, 'Let thanks be given to the Holy Inquisition which commands that this liberty should be corrected.' And in the paintings of Velazquez himself the royal princesses never show their feet.

In Europe generally, during the Middle Ages, shoe fetishism of a different kind manifested itself, not in regard to women's shoes but men's. Nothing is more extraordinary than the extremely elongated shoes worn by men in the fourteenth and fifteenth centuries. Some of these ended merely in a point, and it would hardly seem that this fashion, absurd as it might be, merited the torrent of invective anathema directed against it. But some of these 'poulaines' or 'cracowes', as they were called, terminated in lions' claws, eagles' beaks, and even assumed the very shape of the phallus. This frank expression of shoe fetishism was denounced as *maudit de Dieu* and prohibited by royal ordinance, which proved as ineffective as all sumptuary laws. The phallus-shaped shoe was a true lingam, a combination of male and female attributes, for if the toe of the shoe symbolized the male organ the form of the shoe itself symbolized the vulva.

The long pointed shoe disappeared at the end of the fifteenth century, but shoes still preserved an erotic significance. The first European writer to give evidence of shoe-fetishism in its modern sense was Restif de la Bretonne (1734–1806) who, in his autobiography, *Monsieur Nicolas*, deals with the matter in considerable detail. At the age of four he felt himself attracted to the feet of little girls, and at nine he was 'trembling with pleasure' at the sight of a row of neat little shoes put out for cleaning. As an adolescent he stole the slippers of a young woman older than himself. Later, when apprenticed to a printer, he fell in love with his master's wife, chiefly because, as he tells us, 'she possessed a charm which I could never resist, a pretty little foot. . . . Her shoes, made in Paris, had that voluptuous elegance which seems to communicate soul and life.' One day he saw her wearing rose-coloured shoes with tongues and with green heels and a pretty rosette. They were new and she exchanged them for an equally pretty pair of

114

green slippers with rose heels. When she had left the room he seized the discarded shoes and, 'carried away by the most impetuous passion . . . I seemed to see and touch her in handling what she had just worn; my lips pressed one of these jewels, while the other, deceiving the sacred end of nature, from excess of exultation replaced the object of sex (I cannot express myself more clearly)'. Indeed, it was hardly necessary for him to express himself more clearly. He continued to idolize Madame Parangon (such was the lady's name) and desired that one of her shoes should be buried with him.

Towards the end of the century heels disappeared altogether, and Restif in his old age must surely have regretted the advent of the heelless slippers worn by ladies in the Napoleonic era. Later in the nineteenth century these slippers achieved their own erotic significance by the very difficulty of setting eyes on them. They were, to revive the phrase of the poet Suckling, like 'little mice running in and out'. But in the third quarter of the century heels came in again and have shown a general tendency to go higher ever since. The modern shoe fetishism seems to concentrate on heels so high as to cause acute discomfort to the wearer.

The same might be said of excessive tight-lacing, but of course the whole question is what is meant by excessive. Some kind of waistband has been worn from the earliest times and was thought to give valuable support during active exertion. But it was among the leisure classes in nearly all civilizations that the constriction of the waist was most marked. In ancient Egypt the girdles worn by both sexes were sufficiently tight to be apparently the cause of the remarkably slim waists which are so characteristic a feature of the sculptures and paintings in tombs and palaces. The width of their girdles varied considerably, but they were usually broad and made of linen, and the women appear to have worn two distinct girdles, one high up, immediately below the bosom, and the other placed lower, just above the hip bones. The Semitic races, who derived their civilization mainly from the Egyptians, also wore girdles as part of their ordinary costume, but these do not seem to have been excessively tight. On the other hand, the Cretans, both men and women, had waists so small as to imply a drastic degree of constriction from comparatively early childhood. In ancient Greece a girdle was an essential part of both male and female

115

'Fashion is the comparative of which Fetishism is the superlative.' (Illustrations from the hand-out of a 'personal friendship club'.)

Muslin gowns of 1904.

costume. Herodotus referred to 'a way-girt man', showing that the Greeks recognized the connection between tight waist belts and active muscular exertion. Greek women used several varieties of girdles but their costume does not, in general, include anything which might properly be called 'tight-lacing', and very slender waists never seem to have formed part of the Greek ideal of either male or female beauty.

During the Dark Ages the erotic and æsthetic aspects of dress were, of course, at a discount. But as early as the end of the twelfth century we begin to find references in literature to tight-lacing and, by the end of the thirteenth, a wide belt or bandeau pushed up the bust and narrowly confined the waist, and this tendency was increased in the next one hundred and fifty years. We find the moralists of the period exclaiming equally against the daring décolletage of robes and the excessive narrowness of the waist; and already at the same period we find the first attempts to make the apparent size of the waist still smaller by enlarging the skirt, although there was as yet nothing comparable either with the farthingale of the sixteenth century or the crinoline of the nineteenth.

It is safe to say that nearly all women of the upper classes from the medieval period until the end of the eighteenth century wore some kind of corset. This was not necessarily a detached garment, for the same effect could be produced by stiffening the bodice. In the Elizabethan period this stiffening took the form of a busk, a rigid bar which kept the front of the corsage in position, and this rigid bar was at first so long that it stretched from a point between the breasts to a point very low down on the abdomen, as can be seen very clearly in portraits of Queen Elizabeth. This rigid bar was later replaced

116

by whalebone and the corset thus formed was often laced in front and used as a decorative adjunct to the dress.

Then came the French Revolution and for almost a generation corsets were abandoned, or at least reduced to a kind of brassière or simply to a narrow shawl worn like a scarf across the back like a pair of men's braces. The waist was very high, for it is one of the marks of an epoch of emancipation to have the waist in the wrong place, either very high as in 1800 or low as in 1925. At such periods when the waist is just under the bosom or down at the level of the hips, tight-lacing is obviously impossible, but by 1820 the waist descended once again to its normal position with the inevitable result that it became tighter and tighter. By 1850 it was very tight indeed and medical men began to be concerned about its deleterious effect. But their vain protests must be left to a later chapter.

What concerns us here is the *reason* why many attempts at reform met with such strenuous, and even hysterical, opposition. 'The tightening of the waist girth', says Ernest Crawley, 'is a remarkable adaptation, which emphasizes at one and the same time the feminine characters of expansion both of the breasts and of the abdominal and gluteal regions.' Havelock Ellis makes a further point when he remarks that 'not only does the corset render the breasts more prominent; it has the further effect of displacing the breathing activity of the lungs in an upward direction, the advantage thus gained from the point of view of sexual allurement being that additional attention is drawn to the bosom from the respiratory movement thus imparted to it'.[1]

Tight-lacing, however, was not only a means of inciting breast-fetishism but a fetishism in its own right. Women accepted tight-lacing as they have accepted every dictate of Fashion; it was men who were thrown into a state of excitement by the mere suggestion that it should be relaxed. It is true that they put forward all kinds of seemingly rational arguments in favour of constricting the female waist. It was pointed out that the human body—and especially the female body—needed *some* kind of support, due to its erect posture, and we find the same argument put forward as recently as 1931 by that penetrating sociologist Gerald Heard. He remarks that:

[1] Havelock Ellis. *Studies in the Psychology of Sex.* 1923

we are naturally proud of our upright position, but it has cost us a lot. Even anatomically we are not yet quite natural: there is something artificial about our carriage. Anatomists are always pointing out that the abdominal wall has never evolved sufficient musculature to hold the internal organs as well as they were held when we went crouched. . . . It is no use blinking the fact, even anatomically we are an experimental animal, a building from which you can't safely throw away the scaffolding. So constriction and artificial support are not necessarily unhealthy.[1]

Skirt in 'rustling taffeta' (1906).

Of course, the Victorians who had not yet accepted Darwin would not have liked the reference to the time 'when we went crouched', but otherwise they would have agreed.

The results of a more detailed physiological study by C. S. Roy, Professor of Pathology at Cambridge, and J. Adami, afterwards Vice-Chancellor of Liverpool University, were set forth in a paper read before the British Association in 1888.[2] They maintained that a slight pressure on the abdomen resulted in an increase in the quantity of blood expelled by the heart:

> or, in other words, such pressure diminishes the quantity of blood which is stored in the abdominal veins and venous capillaries, and places more of it at the disposal of the organism as a whole. . . . Pressure on the abdomen, or constriction of the waist, which comes to the same thing, increases therefore the amount of blood placed at the disposal of the muscles, brain, skin, etc.

The two doctors go on to recommend the wearing of a waist-band, belt or corset for both men and women and add that 'the efficacy of such a girdle is not so great when formed of an elastic material, as when it is composed of some comparatively inelastic substance such as leather'.[3]

On the level not of physiology but of sociology it has been pointed out that ages in which women were not tight-laced have been 'loose' in other ways also. The present author, at the beginning of his researches into such matters, noted the 'curious fact of social history . . . that the disappearance of corsets is always accompanied by two related phenomena—promiscuity and an inflated currency. No corsets, bad money and general moral laxity; corsets, sound money, and the prestige of the *grande cocotte*—such seems to be the rule.'

[1] Gerald Heard. 'Why Men Won't Have Dress Reform'. 1937.
[2] Afterwards published in *The National Review*, 1888.
[3] For medical opinion opposed to tight lacing, see Chapter 12.

These, and similar remarks, resulted first in a correspondence with, and later the friendship of, Sir Basil (then Captain B. H.) Liddell Hart who, in a paper written in 1944, says:

> On further reflection, it becomes evident that the corset has a dual quality. It inculcates self-discipline and represents the principle of orderliness. At the same time it enhances attractiveness by accentuating womanly curves and suggesting a concealed softness. In fact, it fulfils the feminine desire to combine opposites—'to have it both ways.' In the occasional intervals when woman has abandoned it she has thus lost it both ways. Women's attractiveness easily degenerates into sloppiness, which saps both attraction and respect.

Be that as it may, there is all the difference in the world between what Drs Roy and Adami call 'a slight pressure on the abdomen' and the really brutal constrictions to which women have submitted in periods when tight-lacing was the vogue. Unfortunately, improvements in corset manufacture enabled the constriction of the waist to be more extreme than ever. It is probable that fashionable women have never been more tightly laced than in the first decade of the present century. Queens and *demi-mondaines* vied with one another in producing a slim waist. The famous Polaire boasted one of seventeen inches and this counted as one of her principal attractions when she appeared on the stage. It is impossible to look at one of her photographs today without a feeling of acute discomfort, even of pain; and this may indeed be the clue to the whole matter. A delight in excessive tight-lacing, like pleasure in excessively high-heeled shoes, is due to an unacknowledged sadism. Sometimes it is not even unacknowledged. The pornographic literature of the period makes no secret of the fact that the pleasure felt in contemplating tight-lacing was directly proportional to the pain inflicted. In some cases there was a double pleasure: sadism in the man who inflicted the pain and masochism in the woman who endured it. What has all this to do with Fashion? Perhaps more than we are always willing to admit. Fashion pushes exaggeration to the point where cruelty begins. Perhaps we might sum it up by saying that Fashion is the comparative of which fetishism is the superlative.

Certainly the erotic-aesthetic of *la Belle Époque* was heavily slanted towards tight-lacing. Its other obsession was underclothes. There was nothing absolutely new in this for already,

A corset of 1908.

119

in the second half of the eighteenth century, artists had penetrated into the feminine boudoir and showed us, in their paintings and prints, the women of the period at all stages of their toilette. *Le Monument du Costume* is a mine of information on such matters, and the story is taken up by the makers of *estampes galantes* whose work continued throughout the earlier part of the nineteenth century. But it was not until the end of the century that underclothes began to be, as it were, deliberately exploited, not only in erotic prints but in the ordinary attire of the fashionable women. In the words of Dr C. Willett Cunnington:

> the breach with Victorian tradition was fundamental. Undergarments became 'lingerie', and their primary function was—to attract the opposite sex. We find them being frankly called 'seductive' (though the meaning is somewhat equivocal), and it is significant that to mark their new functions many of the old names were changed. Drawers became knickers, a chemise became a slip, and the petticoats, in common parlance, 'frillies'.

The underclothes of a woman of the '90s consisted of a linen shift, a pair of very short linen knickers, adorned with ribbon, and over them two or more frilled skirts; but elegant women soon began to tire of simple linen, and at least one of the petticoats began to be made of silk. This had the advantage not only of adding to the luxury of the ensemble, but of giving a curious swishing noise to the movements of the wearer, which contemporary observers no doubt found extremely seductive. This was the famous frou-frou so typical of the period. The fashions of the time which required a bell-shaped effect in the skirt left room for innumerable frills and flounces on the undergarment. It became almost a point of honour with fashionable women to be more glorious within than without; to wear, for example, a very plain tailor-made cloth skirt, and underneath it, glimpsed when the skirt was lifted to cross a street, a wealth of petticoats of extreme fineness and elaboration. In the most elaborate designs the trimming was all concentrated on the lower half of the petticoat. The top was made perfectly plain and tight fitting in order to allow the overdress to lie over the hips as smoothly as possible. And some of these creations were extremely expensive; we hear of 'petticoats at all prices up to £50 each'. Never since the seventeenth century had so much lace been worn. A typical petticoat for evening use might be

120

made of pink satin ornamented by deep flounces of *écru Breton* net, edged by ruching of rose-coloured chiffon. Another model was of yellow brocade, the lower half trimmed with rather deep flounces of black lace, festooned at intervals by the aid of rosettes of yellow ribbon with hanging loops, with a tiny diamond buckle scintillating in the centre of each. One can only wonder what could be the possible use of such elaborate undergarments for a respectable woman, but of course the women who set the tone in such matters were the *grandes cocottes*, then at the height of their prestige and prosperity. As all skirts were long and trailing, it was absolutely necessary to gather them up in the hand when crossing a road, and it was then that the beautiful lace of the underskirt was delicately revealed. This, too, was the period of the Can-Can, a dance which relied for its effect upon the revelation of 'frillies' and 'frothy' underwear.

The top-hat in its prime (1857).

Another focus for fetishism is undoubtedly the hat, for there is indeed something very strange about hats and the forms they have assumed. They appear fairly late in human history. Primitive peoples do not wear hats. Kings have always worn crowns (that is, just the rim of a hat) and savage warriors often wear feathers (that is, the trimmings without the hat itself). Soldiers even in early days wore helmets to turn aside the sword-stroke of an enemy. Ancient Greek shepherds had a large flat hat to keep off the sun but this was really an umbrella, and when they did not need it they wore it on the shoulder. The ancient Romans had no hats at all; they simply covered the head occasionally with a fold of the toga. The notion that men should wear hats whenever they went out of doors is quite a modern idea; in the middle ages they wore hoods; and the notion that women should wear hats at all is more recent still.

Freud implies that the putting on of any hat is a phallic gesture. Certainly when a primitive king put on his crown he was indicating his symbolic marriage to the body politic. The hat is, as it were, a symbol of potent masculinity and it is at least curious that epochs of extreme male domination have coincided with high-hats for men. The high-hat of the Puritans of the seventeenth century is an obvious example. The Cavaliers wore a similar hat but with the addition of the plume, and this might be thought to symbolize mastery with panache. In the nineteenth century it is possible to plot the rise and fall

121

of the curve of feminine emancipation from the height of men's hats. Absolute male domination of, say, 1850 was certainly accompanied by extremely tall hats. With the advent of the New Woman in the 1880s many men adopted the boater, which might be thought of as a very much truncated top-hat. And towards the end of the century men began to wear, so to speak, the very symbol of their bashed-in authority: the trilby hat. This hat meant that men had begun to give up the struggle for domination and to acknowledge women's right to be free. And it is surely no accident that the form of the trilby is the very symbol of *femininity*. If an Indian Yogi with the power of levitation should float over an assembly of men wearing trilby hats, he might well conclude that they represented the Yoni-on-top; and when, in our own age, we have reached the era of complete camaraderie, both sexes give up hats altogether, or at least tend to do so.

For the wearing of hats by women is always a *défi*. When St Paul said that women should remain covered in the churches he was certainly not telling them to wear provocative hats: he was urging them to be decently veiled. Women only began to wear hats when they began to be emancipated. In other words, they have stolen their hats from men. It is true that they have added a lot of trimmings but the basic hat is a trophy won from the male, even when it is as large as the hats of 1780 or 1910 or as small as the hats of 1850 or 1935. On two occasions, in 1780 and again in 1910, very big hats were the prelude to a great social upheaval; they forecast, as it were, a new wave of female emancipation. They were not only a portent, they were a protest. It is obvious that the hats of 1910 were saying something in their symbolic language, and what they were saying was 'Votes for Women'. So does symbolism defeat practicality, for if you are going to fight a policeman it is better to wear a very small hat, or no hat at all. This is what women do when they have won their fight and taken a (temporary or permanent) step forward on the road to emancipation. After a great social upheaval, like the French Revolution or the First World War, women do wear very small hats and these are always a sign of their victory, social upheaval and female emancipation being two sides of the same penny.

But there is one significant exception. If the small hat is not really a hat at all but a *bonnet*, then it is a very different story.

122

The straw boater (1900) ma
decline.

A bonnet is a sign of submission to male authority. It is the nearest thing that modern woman can get to a veil. The bonnets of 1840 are very typical. They are the natural out-door wear of the Victorian submissive woman with her full skirts and flat-heeled slippers. From the defeat of the first Napoleon to the defeat of the third, women wore bonnets, with the significant exception of the romantic '30s, when they let the strings go free (thus transforming their headgear into hats), and metaphorically 'flung their bonnets over the windmills'.

It is a commonplace of costume history that when women are emancipated or feel they are about to be so, they invariably steal some article of male attire: the hat, the coat, the waist-coat and finally the trousers. And very often pioneers of female emancipation have symbolized their militancy by wearing collars and ties.

The tie is an extraordinary example of how a more or less accidental article of clothing can become charged with erotic significance. The history of the evolution of the tie is certainly very curious. There was plainly no place for it in medieval dress nor in the décolleté masculine modes of the Renaissance. The contemporaries of our own Henry VII wore a shirt which exposed the throat. A draw-string was threaded through the top edge and when this was drawn tight we see the beginnings of a ruff. Later in the sixteenth century the frill at the top of the shirt became larger and larger, until the contemporaries of Queen Elizabeth wore round their necks a ruff as big as a dinner plate. However, the string which kept it in place was invisible and can hardly be called a tie. In the middle of the seventeenth century this string or strings reappear at the gap of the neck left by the falling collar. In its turn this collar shrank to a *rabat*, a kind of scarf attached to the shirt and trimmed with lace; and then at last, towards the end of the reign of King Charles II, we see a large bow underneath the falling bands keeping them in place. The word cravat which comes into use at this period is supposed to be derived from the neckwear of the Croatian mercenaries who served in the armies of King Louis XIV. This was fashionable until about 1740, and was worn by older men until a generation later. Younger men wore a stock made of linen or cambric folded to form a high neckband, and when we come to the 1790s we find a kind of neck-cloth indistinguishable from the cravat. In the

The soft beaver hat (1908): dented masculinity.

123

early nineteenth century the dandies set great store by their neck-cloths and many new varieties were introduced.

This neck-cloth finally dwindled in the middle of the century to something we would recognize as a tie. The end could be tied in a bow or left to fall down the middle of the chest and it is here that an erotic symbolism begins to enter. It is a fundamental principle of sympathetic magic that anything that resembles something else becomes identified with it. An obvious example is the cowrie shell which, from its supposed resemblance to the vulva, became thereby a symbol of fertility. In the same way a tie, still on the level of the unconscious mind, has become a symbol of the male organ, and that this is so, fantastic as it may seem, can be deduced from numerous examples. It is well known that youths express their growing consciousness of virility by wearing a loud tie, and sometimes this symbolism is so blatant as to be startling in its implications. American college boys have been known to wear ties embroidered with the figure of a naked woman or, by an extraordinary sophistication, a woman who is clothed by daylight but naked by artificial light. A prostitute is quoted as saying 'I never stop a gentleman with a crumpled tie'; and it is notorious that the Lesbian type of woman almost invariably wears a tie. It is presumably in accordance with the same unconscious symbolism that parsons do not wear ties. Half a century ago the old-fashioned Evangelical clergyman did wear a tie, but it was always white, as if to indicate that he was 'potent but pure'. But if a minister of any denomination is any kind of imitation of a Roman Catholic priest, he does not wear a tie: that is, he is symbolically castrated. In Paris there was until recently a certain night-club where each male guest was compelled to sing a song. If he did not do so to the satisfaction of those present the hostess approached him with a large pair of scissors and cut off his tie. The roars of laughter with which this action was greeted was sufficient indication of the unconscious emotion which this produced.

So much for what might be called the Freudian significance of ties; we must now turn to the Adlerian meaning, for if ties on the one hand express the Lust of the Eye, on the other hand, they certainly represent the Pride of Life, i.e. the Hierarchical Principle. One has only to think of the 'old school tie', to see that this is true. Some scholars have thought that in the school or regimental tie, there is a faint echo of the 'colours' which the medieval knight carried into battle, but perhaps this is stretching a theory of historical continuity to breaking point. All the same, a meaningful tie is, just as much as the blazon on a shield, an example of man's need of symbolism. We suffer in the modern world, as Jung has pointed out, from 'an unparalleled impoverishment of symbolism'. As far as modern men's clothes are concerned, the tie might be regarded as its last refuge; and this may explain the victory of the long tie over the bow tie, the former offering a larger field for symbolic colouring or emblems. We can note its emergence towards the end of the 1860s, but in the early years coats were buttoned so high that there was little space for significant display. In the '70s the opening at the top of the waistcoat became wider and wider and fancy ties in stripes and spots began to appear, although these at first were dictated only by personal fancy.

It is perhaps no accident that the tie which means something comes into existence about the same time as the blazer. There has been much controversy about the origin of blazers, but it seems certain that they were worn in the early '80s by undergraduates at Oxford and Cambridge who belonged to rowing or cricket clubs. A caricature of a young man watching cricket shows him wearing a striped blazer, a striped cap and a striped tie, and it seems likely that all three represented the same 'colours'. It is in this development that sociologists and psychologists might find a rewarding field for their inquiries. For just at the time when men's ordinary clothes had assumed a universal drabness, they chose to break into colour for clothes for sport; but it was not only lack of colour they were suffering from but a lack of ritual meaning; for if man is by nature ritualistic, how poverty-stricken indeed was the English gentleman of the second half of the nineteenth century!

It is true that the new 'High Church' party was endeavouring to bring back pomp and colour into the ceremonies of the Anglican Church, but the average Englishman regarded these innovations with dislike and contempt. There was, therefore, no escape for him in this direction. Nor could he feast his eyes any longer on the gorgeousness of military uniform, for it was just at this period (the early 1880s) that the British army abandoned its red tunics, to the disgust of the marksmen who

125

had found them such excellent targets in the First Boer War. With the Church and the Army no longer satisfying his need for colour and for symbolism, and with the small possibility before him of becoming a mayor, a High Court judge or a Doctor of Divinity, there was only one route left open to him —sport. And as far as ties are concerned, it does seem likely that the first tie to mean something meant, 'I belong to the Oxford University Boat Club', or something of the kind.

Sport in Britain in the last quarter of the nineteenth century was largely the affair of the universities and public schools and so, by a natural development, the idea of the symbolic tie was adopted by these institutions. Wellington College, founded in 1853, had a rugger XV which shortly began to play in orange-and-black-barred jerseys, and a cricket XI which sported light-blue caps piped with yellow. These colours, curiously—but appropriately—enough were taken from the ribbon of the Crimean War medal. They are now embodied in the school tie.

This transference of already accepted colours to a tie is perhaps most readily seen in regimental ties. Before the days of universal khaki all regiments had a colour scheme of their own, seen at its most typical in the mess-jackets of the officers. Cynics have suggested that many of these colours were probably suggested by the colonel's wife, 'because they looked pretty'. Nevertheless, it does seem that with certain army units, and especially rifle regiments, some of the colours once used for their full dress uniforms have been perpetuated in their regimental ties. Obvious examples include the striped red and green of the King's Royal Rifle Corps (uniform: rifle green with scarlet facings); the black and green stripes of the Rifle Brigade (full dress: green with black facings). The same could be said of the grey, black and white stripes of the tie of the Artists' Rifles and the green and blue stripes of the Inns of Court Regiment. The proliferation of ties down to the level of suburban bowling clubs meant that the old school tie became something of a joke. Today it is safe to say that men who have been to the more famous public schools do not in general wear old school ties. The interesting exception is Eton, which happens to have a particularly attractive one. Old Wykehamists sometimes wear scarves in the colours of Winchester school but few of them wear the tie: it is just too hideous.

The question of the hierarchical element in the old school

126

tie has taken us rather far from the subject of this present chapter, but perhaps it is important to remember that the Hierarchical Principle is seldom entirely absent even when clothes and accessories have a more obvious erotic interest. Perhaps we might sum up the whole question by saying that the old school tie is not only a fetish but a totem.

Children

Should be Seen . . .

10

The Reverend Isaac Watts, writing his plain-spoken hymns for children in the early eighteenth century, brusquely demanded:

Why should the garments made to hide
Our parents' shame provoke our pride?

Such questions must have provoked a certain confusion in infants' minds, and in the minds of adults also. For it is undoubtedly true that for long periods of human history one of the objects of children's costume (at least in the upper classes) was to maintain, if not to provoke, a certain pride in dress, i.e. to indicate to the world at large the social status of the parents. This is the Hierarchical Principle all over again.

But here the Seduction Principle operates in reverse; for all respectable parents were anxious that their children, especially their female children, should not be conscious of sexual impulses too early. The attractions of very young girls should be damped down for as long as possible. The Utility Principle, i.e. providing clothes in which it was possible for children to play, never seems to have entered into anybody's calculations until the middle of the eighteenth century.

In primitive communities, of course, the question does not arise: children are left to run about naked until the age of puberty. Indeed, the attitude of all savage societies to children was permissive in the extreme. They were never beaten; and missionaries have sometimes in the past found themselves in considerable danger from the adult members of the tribe when they have presumed to 'correct' the pupils in their schools by methods accepted without question at Eton and Harrow.

Géza Róheim, who had enormous experience as a field anthropologist, controverts the opinion of previous writers that severe education is necessarily correlated with patriarchy and tolerant education with matriarchy. But he admits that savage

The Old Pretender and his sister, by
N. de Larguillière (National Portrait
Gallery, London).

children have a very good time by comparison with civilized
children. Savages are not 'nervous' and do not mind noise;
nor do they mind if their children indulge in those activities
which the psycho-analysts designate 'fore-pleasure'.

> It is interesting to observe [he says] how the jealousy of the old
> towards the young has continually widened its sphere during the
> course of evolution. This is mirrored in endo-psychic life by the
> spread of reference *from end-pleasure to fore-pleasure*. Until puberty,
> all merely playful sexual behaviour of monkeys and apes occurs
> without provoking any aggression from the adults. The analogy
> with the behaviour of primitive peoples, especially the Australians,
> is striking, the almost complete freedom of youth being in marked
> contrast with the persecutions and educational endeavours of the
> puberty rites. The higher the society, the earlier the education,
> that is, the more serious the attitudes of adults towards infantile
> sexuality and the greater the tendency to repress it. . . . Severe
> educators . . . are people who, suffering from a sense of guilt them-
> selves, punish themselves vicariously in the persons of their
> children. Jealous adults, and the super-egos which are their
> shadows, first prohibit end-pleasure and then the pre-genital forms
> of pleasure. When masturbation and excretory functions have
> become 'not nice' we have reached a high stage of culture.[1]

The Ancient Egyptians had reached a high stage of culture
and may have had their own ideas about what was 'not nice'.
But nudity was certainly not included; for when we look at
Egyptian wall-paintings we can see that not only the servants
but the young princesses wore no clothes at all. The Ancient
Greeks had a similar attitude, for although boys and girls were
provided with simple garments, they invariably took them off

[1] Géza Róheim. *The Riddle of the Sphinx.* 1934.

129

when exercising in the gymnasium. After all, that is what the word 'gymnasium' means. The Greeks had no horror of the body.

Such horror seems to have been a Semite peculiarity, for the young in Assyrian bas-reliefs are almost as much bedizened with fringed shawls as their elders. By way of the Jews this Semite attitude was carried over into Christianity and the condition of children deteriorated still further for another reason also. The doctrine of Original Sin made it seem as if there were something regrettable in being a child at all. Parents and grown-up people generally were supposed to have overcome their natural tendencies to evil, and so were never tired of pointing out to the young that there was only one way for rational beings to behave, and that was to imitate their elders as closely as possible. The natural corollary was that they should dress like their elders, and so, for many hundreds of years, they did.

From this rule the Dark Ages provided a happy exception. When the greater part of the world reverted to barbarism, the children of peasants were once more free to run about naked. They probably did so in this country at least into Anglo-Saxon times; but when the records become plentiful again at the end of the Middle Ages, we find little notion of a special dress for children. In the sixteenth, seventeenth and eighteenth centuries it was taken for granted that the children of those who could afford the expense should resemble miniature replicas of their parents. This was certainly true of the girls and the older boys, but with younger boys the case was slightly different. The tendency to dress young boys as girls is found all over the world, and was operative in our own country as late as the beginning of the present century, if in a modified degree. The present writer has a photograph of himself in petticoats at an age when the little boy of today would certainly have been 'breeched'.

Anthropologists seem to think that the reason for this was the quaint notion that the evil spirits menacing the life of young children thought more highly of boys than of girls and were therefore more eager to do them injury. But the spirits were also stupid enough to be deceived by feminine or semi-feminine garments and so were induced to leave the boys alone. It is hard for us to think ourselves back into the state of mind which this implies, but it certainly influenced the costume of male

130

Post-Rousseau
children's clothes,
1787.

children for many generations. King Louis XIV wore skirts until long after babyhood; and to this day some of the male peasant costumes of Holland show feminine elements persisting until the age of about twelve.

Apart from this curious aberration, the rule holds good that the children of the upper classes, at least in Western Europe, were dressed as replicas of their elders until the middle of the eighteenth century. Perhaps little girls suffered most. From the tenderest years their delicate bodies were encased in boned corsets; sometimes they were compelled to sleep in them in order that in later life they might have the slender waist which was so much admired. Small wonder that they grew up languid and listless even if they were lucky enough to escape curvature of the spine. Boys did not suffer from that particular restriction, but no healthy young male could possibly enjoy being rigged out in silk stockings, satin breeches and embroidered coat. Perhaps the sword at the side was the only part of the get-up the boys liked.

Before the second half of the eighteenth century, therefore, the eccentricities of children's dress are a reflection of the eccentricities of grown-up attire. The square shoes and enormous sleeves of Henry VIII were worn by boys also, once they had put away petticoats. The upper-class young Elizabethan had his neck encased in a ruff, while his sister's body was squeezed with a busk and grotesquely extended by a farthingale. Did the grown-up Cavalier drip with lace, his younger contemporary was almost as bedizened, and at the end of the seventeenth century little girls were given a 'fontange' or top-knot almost as tall as those of their mothers.

The coming of the periwig in the reign of Charles II brought in a new problem. How strange it is that, for a century after 1670, every civilized man in Europe shaved off his own hair and put on a wig, sometimes of gigantic proportions! Here at least boys did have a certain advantage, for in general they were allowed to keep their own hair dressed to resemble a wig and even, sometimes, dusted with powder. Little girls, less fortunate, had no sooner got rid of the towering head-dresses of Queen Anne's reign than they were required to assume the hoops and panniers of the following fashion.

One of the first to protest against these absurdities was the philosopher John Locke in his *Thoughts Concerning Education.*

He was particularly severe on the practice of swaddling infants, an almost universal custom in the early years of the eighteenth century. The unfortunate child was wrapped up like a parcel and tightly bound so that it was impossible to move the limbs. A generation later, swaddling was being more and more given up and towards the end of the century had disappeared. A doctor, writing in *The Lady's Magazine* in 1785, was able to say that 'the barbarous custom of swathing children like living mummies, is now almost universally laid aside'.

By that time too there had been a real revolution in the clothing of older children, and the credit for this is generally given to Rousseau. It was in 1762 that, having a dozen years before startled the polite world by his defence of the 'noble savage', he brought out his novel *Émile*. It is more of a treatise than a novel, as the sub-title, *De l'Éducation*, shows, and in it Rousseau proclaimed the theory, far more startling in the eighteenth century than it would be today, that the untutored child is often a nobler being than one who has been subjected to the rigours of a conventional upbringing.

The proposition is debatable, but at least it had the good effect of suggesting to the parents and educationists of the day that *perhaps* children might be considered as having needs quite different from those of mature persons. No doubt it was all part of the general movement of Romanticism, part of the sensibility which was becoming increasingly the fashion, part of the impulse which led Marie Antoinette to dress up as a milkmaid and pretend to tend the cows at the Petit Trianon. At all events, it led to a considerable modification—a rationalization, as we might call it—of children's dress.

There is a painting by Zoffany of the family of Lord Willoughby de Broke in the 1770s. It shows the family at tea, and the interesting thing about it is that, while the father and mother are still eighteenth-century figures in silks and satins and with powdered hair, the children are dressed in rather flimsy white garments with a simple sash set rather high. This is the strangest anticipation of the clothes which were to come into fashion at the very end of the century. Then grown-up women abandoned the elaborate clothes of the *Ancien Régime* and assumed the dress (as they thought) of the Ancient Greeks. The dresses of the little girls in Zoffany's picture anticipate grown-up fashions by a whole generation.

Something very similar happened to boys. It is an odd thought that it was the grown-up men in the 1770s and '80s who wore breeches and the boys who wore *trousers*. It is difficult to understand the stigma which at this period of history was still attached to trousers. Trousers were the garb of rough fellows like sailors and of the lower classes generally. The term of contempt, *sans-culottes*, hurled at the *canaille* of France by the aristocrats, did not imply that 'without breeches' meant that the men of the people were wearing the kilt. It meant that they were wearing trousers. Trousers took a long time to shake off this association and it was boys, therefore, who broke down the barrier, for they were undoubtedly wearing trousers long before the *sans-culottes* of the French Revolution had been heard of. If one cannot call this an eccentricity of children's dress, it is certainly an eccentricity in the history of costume.

In the closing years of the eighteenth century the fashion plate, properly so-called, came into existence, and from then on we have a year-to-year record of changing fashion both for children and grown-ups. As we have seen, children's clothes, under the influence of Rousseau, were essentially practical clothes—that is, they were more suitable for an active life than the clothes of grown-ups.

At the beginning of the nineteenth century, clothes for both boys and girls were really sensible—much more sensible than they were afterwards to become. The boys had loose, light-coloured garments, open at the throat; the girls had dresses, the only fault of which was that they were too long. But such a happy condition of affairs was not destined to last.

By the end of the '30s boys' clothes had become tighter and less comfortable again. The usual costume consisted of long trousers and a spencer', or short coat without tails. It is known to us as the short coat with rows of buttons worn by page-boys, and in its other fossilized form as the Eton jacket. But what we know as the Eton collar, enclosing the necks of small boys in a stiff wall of starched linen, was happily still in the future. Little boys of the early Victorian period often wore a collar which was the same in form but larger, looser and more floppy. It must have been much more comfortable than its descendant. Long trousers were universal. The legs even of the very young were not exposed to view.

If the legs of boys could not be exposed, still less could the legs

134

The 'Eton suit', *c*. 1830 and 18

of girls, and this convention led to one of the most extraordinary eccentricities of children's dress ever perpetrated: the preposterous 'pantalettes'. Those of us who have already passed our half century probably made our first acquaintance with these absurd garments in some early illustrated edition of *Uncle Tom's Cabin*. Little Eva wore short if ample skirts and below these her legs could be seen encased in linen tubes edged with lace.

The extremely scanty dresses of the Empire period made some kind of divided garment for women inevitable, although their introduction was fiercely resisted by moralists who implied that any woman who deigned to wear such garments was probably, as the odd phrase has it, no better than she should be. But by the 1830s, most women were wearing lace-trimmed drawers, although these were, of course, invisible under their long skirts. The strange thing is that while the skirts of little girls were shorter than those worn by their mothers, their drawers were not, so that they looked as if they were wearing trousers underneath. It was happily hidden from them that they were thus anticipating the 'reforms' of the redoubtable Mrs Bloomer.

There was certainly an element of snobbery in this, as only wealthy parents could afford to keep their daughters in spotless linen which was all too easily dirtied. The present author has a photograph (it must have been one of the earliest) of his grandmother as a little girl with one of her young friends. My grandmother is not wearing pantalettes, but her little friend is. This probably implied some slight difference in social status.

However, mothers on the borderline of gentility had no need to despair. There were false pantalettes (indeed, it is probable that these were the objects to which the word 'pantalette' is most properly applied) and these were simply cloth tubes trimmed with lace and tied on above the knee.

The other thing which strikes us as odd in the clothes worn by girls in the '40s is the extreme degree of décolletage allowed. There was, of course, no question of 'evening dress' for children: little girls wore the Victorian off-the-shoulder line in the daytime. This is even stranger when we reflect that, below the waist, the female body at all ages had never been more warmly clad. By the early '50s it had become the fashion to wear a great many petticoats of which at least one was of red flannel.

Boy wearing 'Pantalettes'.

135

Modesty in Dress

The crinoline when it was first invented (it became fashionable in the middle '50s) was a great emancipation, for it enabled both women and girls to attain the fashionable silhouettes of wide-spreading skirts without the necessity of a multiplicity of petticoats underneath. But, of course, the crinoline, like all the devices of fashion, got out of hand and by 1860 the hoop-distended skirts were so immense that two women could not enter a room together or sit on the same sofa.

The crinoline was universally worn: by grand ladies, by servants, by actresses—no matter what the supposed period of the play—and by little girls. The little girls had one advantage: when they wore the crinoline they were at least saved, owing to the comparative shortness of their skirts, from the ever-present danger of being burned to death, by the wide, distended flounces catching in the open fires of the period.

It is strange to think that the abandonment in the late 1860s of so absurd a fashion as the crinoline should have meant, as far as girls were concerned, a change for the worse. But so it was. The bustle of the early '70s was an even less practical garment, for it pulled the skirt tightly back over the hips to bunch it up at the back, and so impeded the full use of the limbs. A little girl in a crinoline could at least run about freely inside her swaying cage, but a little girl in a bustle could hardly move at all. Clothes altogether were made tighter and the neckline much more closely fitting. And instead of the rather charming heelless slippers of a previous period, childish feet were confined in tight, high button boots. The hats were much less comfortable than those of the previous decade. Another more serious matter was the return of excessive tight-lacing, even for the young.

All these aberrations, however, are the eccentricities of grown-up dress, reflected more or less completely in the clothes of children. But now we have to consider another element adding to the oddity of juvenile attire. There had been 'fancy dress' for children, on special occasions, from the period when people began to be conscious that the clothes of their own time and country were not the clothes of all time and of every country. Such a notion took a surprisingly long time to find acceptance, for even in the Elizabethan age 'long ago' meant almost inevitably the Romans, and 'far away' the Turks. Fancy dress meant either one or the other. Even as late as the

136

'Our parents are rich.'

second half of the eighteenth century this idea persisted.

There is a charming painting by Zoffany showing Queen Charlotte, wife of George III, at her dressing-table. Two little boys, the future Prince Regent and the future Duke of York, stand beside her. The former is dressed as a miniature Julius Cæsar and the latter as a little Turk. In view of their subsequent history it ought, perhaps, to have been the other way round.

Gainsborough's 'Blue Boy', on the other hand, was dressed in a kind of Cavalier costume, and such clothes were, apparently, not only worn on special occasions. The costumes of the children of rich and sophisticated parents were often, as it were, deliberately 'out of period'. This curious use of 'historical costume' never affected little girls very much. Their dresses nearly always followed the adult mode as closely as possible. It was on their small sons that doting mothers lavished their romantic fancies.

The enthusiasm for the Waverley novels put many a small boy into Scottish cap and tartan kilt, however 'Sassenach' he might be. Byron's fame resulted in a fashion for the Oriental, and after the Crimean War, Young Hopeful might well be got up as a Turco or a Zouave. Towards the end of the century sailor suits became common, and indeed lasted until the First World War. The present author can remember that he spent most of his childhood in a sailor suit.

Boys' suits, last decade of the nineteenth century.

The aesthetic movement of the '80s was not without its effect on children's clothes, and for girls at least the modifications introduced by the swooning mammas of 'Passionate Brompton' were probably all to the good. The fashionable misses of the '80s were done up like parcels, hardly able to move and much too tightly laced: the aesthetic young ladies wore looser garments, some of which were not without their charm. We can gain some notion of them from the drawings of Kate Greenaway, a delicate and talented illustrator, but not (as Ruskin contended) as great an artist as Michelangelo!

The sons of aesthetic parents were less fortunate. We know what many of the adult aesthetes looked like from the caricatures by George Du Maurier in *Punch*, and also from the figure of Bunthorne, still to be seen in revivals of Gilbert and Sullivan's *Patience*. Velvet coat and breeches, with a floppy collar—such were the accepted marks of artistic sensibility; Oscar Wilde wore something of the sort when he went lecturing in America. The

137

juvenile version was usually known as the Little Lord Fauntleroy and was surely calculated to fill any normal boy compelled to wear it with acute embarrassment.

The clothes of non-aesthetic boys (if the phrase may be permitted) showed a distinct change for the worse in the last quarter of the nineteenth century. The jackets became tighter and more tailored. The frilled soft collar turned back over the jacket was abandoned in favour of the stiff Eton collar, or of the stand-up collar imitated from that of grown men. A hard-rimmed topper or bowler hat replaced the softer headgear of the '50s and '60s, and there was a general stiffening and tightening of all male attire, from which even young boys did not escape. Even the much more sensible Norfolk jacket and knickerbockers was spoiled for comfort by the addition of the stiff white Eton collar. This was so easily crumpled and dirtied that economical parents began to substitute celluloid for linen, but this did not add to the wearer's comfort.

It is strange that the activities of the 'New Woman' in the '80s had so little influence on female costume. There was much talk of Emancipation, but emancipated clothes were more grotesque than practical and, as men were admired as more emancipated, women seized on such unessentials of male attire as the stiff collar and added it to their other encumbrances. The new passion for cycling put some young women into knickerbockers, but children did not cycle in those days and so the craze had little effect on the dress of young girls.

The new century brought little improvement; in fact, girls' dresses of the Edwardian period were marked by an extreme of elaboration, even to the absurdly over-bedizened hats. In our modern egalitarian world we have forgotten that cleanliness itself was once prized as a class-distinction with the curious result that well-to-do people tended to wear and to provide for their children clothes which were very easily dirtied. Some little girls, especially in smart circles in Paris in the years before the First World War, were walking advertisements that their parents were able to devote the services of a laundry-maid to them alone.

English girls, on the other hand, until they 'came out' suffered from another kind of tyranny: the school uniform. This usually consisted of an austere white blouse, a 'gym slip', long black stockings, flat-heeled shoes and a stiff straw hat with a

138

ribbon in the school colours round the crown. The hat was usually very wide in the brim and seems to have been modelled on the straw hat worn by the boys of Harrow. The whole outfit was deliberately made as unattractive as possible. Most schoolgirls hated it; but it is interesting to find so acute an observer as Lawrence Langner contrasting it favourably with the clothes worn by schoolgirls in America.

> In the United States, young girls at a fairly early age use lipstick and rouge and ape the dresses of mature women. Compare this with the usual behaviour of young girls of the same age in England, British colonies and other countries, where lipstick and rouge are taboo, and a plain school uniform is generally worn. Consequently, young girls tend to mature more slowly and grow to womanhood without a hot-house forcing of their emotions.[1]

Children's clothes, *c.* 1860.

The movement to provide sensible clothes for children did not really gather momentum until the early '20s. Owing to the difficulty of obtaining starch during the war, the soft-collared shirt was adopted by both men and boys. The very practical shorts with bare knees, almost unknown before the war except for Boy Scouts, now became universal wear for boys up to eleven or twelve. Some public schools, like Radley, had the sense to adopt a school uniform of grey flannel shorts and jackets. Girls' school uniforms grew less hideous and the absurd straw hat was usually abandoned for the 'panama'. Very young children of both sexes were put into rompers. Some nursery schools even reverted to the complete nudity of early times, and neither morals nor health suffered any notable decline. Children of today should be grateful for this at least: that their clothes are now designed chiefly for their own convenience and comfort, and not to display the social status of their parents or to indicate the 'artistic' tastes of their doting mothers. Parents, too, should be grateful not only for a diminution of laundry bills but for the disappearance of all those nervous crises in the nursery which were directly due to the practice of dressing children up in clothes unsuitable for their years.

[1] Lawrence Langner. *The Importance of Wearing Clothes*. 1959.

11 It is surprising that more attention has not been given by historians of costume to the question of sports clothes. Of course, for long periods of time there was nothing that would be recognized as such. Greek maidens sometimes ran races in abbreviated tunics but, for the most part, the Greeks exercised their bodies without any clothes at all. In the medieval period people played games in their ordinary clothes —unless we call tilting armour a special costume for sport.

During the last hundred years sports clothes have acted as a liberating influence on the dress of both men and women, but to a very different degree. Women's sports clothes are, strictly speaking, an irrelevance. They are deviations from the main line of development, they have little or no influence on women's clothes as such. A sports outfit for women is—a 'sport', in the biological sense of the word. But men's sports clothes play an integral part in the evolution of men's ordinary wear. Indeed, without a 'theory of the sports coat' it is impossible to understand the evolution of male attire.

In their primitive form sports clothes are simply *rough* clothes, or country clothes. Sensible men, at any time, do not go hunting or shooting in a costume suitable for appearing at Court. They adopt simpler garments, similar in many ways to the working clothes of the lower classes. Nevertheless, sports clothes began, early in their history, to show important deviations from working clothes.

One might put it another way and say that working clothes, as such, have no influence on fashion. They can obtain such influence only by becoming sports clothes: that is, by showing quite clearly that they are designed for play and not for work. Once the stigma of work is removed, the clothes worn for active pursuits do have an influence on men's fashions: in fact, there

Woman's riding habit, *c.* 1870

140

is nothing else that has any influence. All change in men's dress seems to be effected by adopting a sports costume for 'ordinary wear', and making it darker and less comfortable in the process.

The most obvious example of such evolution is the cutaway riding coat. The English country gentleman of the early years of George III spent much of his time hunting. Even the grandest nobles did not, like their French counterparts, spend their time fluttering round a Court: they spent it on their country estates, and in the saddle. And they soon found that the accepted aristocratic wear of the period, with its skirted and embroidered coat, its white silk stockings and three-cornered hat, was not a practical outfit for the hunting field. So they made the coat of plain cloth with a square slice cut out at the front so as to sit a horse more easily, wore boots instead of buckled shoes and did away with the lace ruffles at throat and wrist. The three-cornered hat had brims too wide and a crown too low; so the brims were shrunk to almost nothing and the crown raised. This was the first crash-helmet—and the ancestor of all top-hats.

The men who made the French Revolution were great admirers of all things English—the anglomania of the period is notorious—and as a sign of their admiration and as a repudiation of the *Ancien Régime* they adopted English clothes— English country clothes. Thus, by the early years of the nineteenth century, what had been sports clothes had become the ordinary wear of fashionable men both in London and Paris. By 1840 these clothes had taken another step to formality by becoming 'evening dress', and going black in the process. There they have remained, fossilized, ever since.

Until 1850, riding was the sport usually practised by gentlemen and almost the only sport indulged in by gentlewomen. Riding habits are therefore the earliest sports clothes for women. They represent a *masculinization* of female costume, but instead of doing this in the obvious way, they are a striking example of what might be called 'sentimental displacement'. The sensible thing, the utilitarian thing, would have been to masculinize the lower half of female costume and to give the woman riding breeches. Instead, the skirt was retained and made so ample that it almost touched the ground when the wearer was mounted (as can be seen quite clearly in equestrian statues of Queen Victoria) and made it almost impossible for her to

Woman's riding habit, *c.* 1954.

141

dismount without the help of a groom. On the other hand, the upper part of the costume (where it did not matter) was made as masculine as possible. Women's sports clothes in their early forms always show this masculine trend *in unessentials*. The earliest women cyclists, for example, thought it necessary to wear stiff white collars and men's hats.

By the middle of the century riding had rivals in other sports. Cricket had been played by gentlemen in the eighteenth century and by the time of the Regency had become quite fashionable. This was a period when men wore white trousers in summer. They also wore white shirts, and when they had taken off their coats and waistcoats—which is all they did at the beginning—they presented much the same appearance as a modern cricket team, except that they did not mind exposing their braces (which was later considered a very vulgar thing to do) and played the game in the vast top-hats of the period. Cricket caps and blazers do not appear until much later. Cricket, too, has hardened into ritual, and so cricket clothes have remained fixed ever since.

Rowing was at first practised in the same costume. The earliest Oxford and Cambridge boat races were rowed in long white trousers, white shirts and top-hats. But trousers are not well suited to rowing—they get too tight over the knee—and in the end common sense prevailed and rowing men began to wear shorts. They also abandoned their top-hats. Shorts, however, were adopted with some reluctance owing to the Victorian complex about the exposure of naked flesh. They had a hard fight with knickerbockers even on the football field. As recently as the '80s footballers usually wore knickerbockers, and when they did begin to wear shorts these were, in general, ludicrously long. The jersey, plain or striped, was finally substituted for the shirt as being more suitable for the rough and tumble round the ball.

Men who wished for something less vigorous and were also unwilling to forgo the company of women had, in the '60s, two gentlemanly pastimes open to them: archery and croquet. Both were engaged in in the ordinary summer clothes of the day, the men in plaid trousers and the women in crinolines. In the next decade came tennis.

This was not, of course, 'real' tennis, the game played with a small ball in a covered court, which had been played by

Englishmen since the fourteenth century and at which Henry VIII and (rather surprisingly) Charles II displayed such skill. It was never played by ladies. The new game was called lawn tennis or, more pedantically, Sphairistike. It was taken up by the fashionable Prince's Club where, as a contemporary chronicler notes, 'away on an extra lawn on the London side of the ground—away from the cricket, away from the mock ice and real ices—away from the skirts and the bugle-embroidered bodies [we would say "bodices"], from the colour, the costumes, and the fashionable crowd, they are playing "Sphairistike" or "lawn tennis".'

Tennis costume, 1885.

It is interesting to note that in 1875 some ground at Wimbledon that had been used for croquet since 1869 was set aside for lawn tennis. The first Wimbledon Lawn Tennis Championship meeting was held in 1877. Two hundred spectators paid a shilling each for admission.

Tennis costume, 1906.

Lawn tennis rapidly became popular, although there was some prejudice against it as a game for men. Schoolmasters referred to it contemptuously as 'pat ball', but this only helped to recommend it to ladies. It was considered a refined game, and it fitted happily into the open-air summer life of the English middle classes. It could be played on a lawn of comparatively moderate size, and it provided a new opportunity (previously only enjoyed by croquet) for that parade of marriageable daughters which was one of the main preoccupations of the British matron. What could be more desirable than a game that could be practised without great expense, which brought young people together and which enabled them to make friends under the eyes of their elders?

In the early days the costumes worn by both men and women had not yet become stereotyped. At Wimbledon in 1887 some of the men played in long white trousers, and a considerable proportion of them wore white flannel knickerbockers with black stockings. Women played in the summer dresses of the day; but these in the 1870s and 1880s were extremely tight in the skirt. *Punch*, in 1877, offered the suggestion that men should be handicapped while playing by having scarves tied round their knees. A bustle was considered necessary for women tennis players almost until the end of the century and even after the bustle had vanished the game was still played in a tight corset and a long trailing skirt. In the middle 1890s, the tennis

143

blouse had enormous balloon sleeves. Also, only too often, the costume was completed by an elaborate befeathered or beflowered hat. The game, as can well be imagined, was by no means as strenuous as it has since become.

At the beginning of the new century, well-known actresses began to be photographed in their gardens 'ready for lawn tennis'. A photograph of Miss Marie Studholme, which appeared in *The Sketch* in 1901, shows the lady in a long dark-coloured skirt, a white blouse with long sleeves and a very fancy lace collarette, and on her head an immense hat covered with a veil of white lace. Many women, however, were by this time wearing 'gent's boaters' and, in order to feel more masculine still, they adopted the stiff white male collar of the period.

It became more and more usual to wear white. Mrs Fenwick, who won the Ladies' Championship in 1908, was entirely clothed in white, but her skirt was extremely full and swirling, and her sleeves were so long that they almost concealed the hands. By 1912 the fullness of skirts had disappeared even in ordinary wear and tennis modes followed suit, except that they were sensibly shorter. The hobble skirt never made its appearance on the tennis court, for the very sufficient reason that it would have been impossible to play in it at all. This was a stage in the establishment of a definite costume for tennis, for sports clothes always take a step forward when they diverge from ordinary costume.

Mrs Lambert Chambers in 1919 was still playing in a long skirt and a blouse with long sleeves; but, in the same year, there flashed into the sky a woman who was to revolutionize the whole conception of a suitable dress for tennis. Her name was Suzanne Lenglen. Lord Aberdare, in his *The Story of Tennis*, tells us all about it.

> Suzanne acquired strength and pace of shot by playing with men, and for playing a man's type of game she needed freedom of movement. Off came the suspender belt, and she supported her stockings by means of garters above the knee; off came the petticoat and she wore only a short pleated skirt; off came the long sleeves and she wore a neat short-sleeved vest. Her first appearance at Wimbledon caused much comment, but the success of her outfit led to its adoption by others. In her first championship, she had worn a white hat but on subsequent occasions she wore a brightly

144

Ancient Roman girl (Mansell Collection).

coloured bandeau which was outstandingly popular until challenged by Miss Helen Wills's eyeshade in 1924.

Suzanne herself offered the following advice:

If you wish to look neat in court, never wear a coloured skirt, always a white one. . . . I will briefly detail what I consider the ideal dress: a simple *piqué* dress, or one of drill or linen, made in the old Grecian style, and fastened at the waist with a ribbon or leather belt. The sleeves should be short.

By the end of 1925 ordinary day dresses were short, but five years later they had become long again. It seemed absurd for tennis dresses to do the same, although quite long models were offered to the public as late as 1934. Most women, however, had no wish to return to hampering draperies, and in 1931 Señorita de Alvarez played in divided skirts that came to slightly below the knee. Two years later Miss Alice Marble appeared in shorts above the knee. The new mode received great impetus from the example of Mrs Fearnley Whittingstall and Miss Kathleen Stammers, whose extreme elegance in these garments induced a host of women to follow their example. It was Mrs Fearnley Whittingstall who, playing at Forest Hills, in America, first appeared on the courts with bare legs.

Men, strangely enough, took some time to catch up. But in 1949 all the male competitors at Wimbledon wore shorts. Tennis dress for both sexes would seem to have reached its final term.

The history of bathing costumes is very curious, for, after all, the only sensible costume for bathing in is no costume at all. The Greeks and Romans would have thought it madness to put on clothes in order to get them wet. In the Middle Ages both sexes bathed together naked in the bath houses in spite of the strictness of the Church, which regarded such institutions as little better than brothels. At Bath in the reign of Charles II the bathers were more self-conscious, and thanks to a work entitled *The Journeys of Celia Fiennes* we have a detailed picture of the contemporary scene.

The Ladye [she says] goes into the bath with garments made of a fine yellow canvas, which is stiff and made large with great sleeves like a parson's gown, the water fills it up so that its borne off that your shape is not seen. . . . the Gentlemen have drawers and wastcoates of the same sort of canvas, this is the best linning, the bath water will change any other yellow; when you go out of

145

Bathing costumes, *c.* 1880.

Mid-1930s.

the bath you go within a doore that leads to steps which you ascend . . . and let your canvass drop off by degrees into the water . . . meanetyme your maide flings a garment of flannell made like a nightgown with great sleeves over your head, and the guides take the taile and so pulls it on you just as you rise the steps, and your other garment drops off so you are wrapped in the flannell and your nightgown on top, your slippers, and so you are set in Chaire which is brought into the roome . . .

In the late eighteenth century people began to bathe in the sea: a 'watering place' ceased to be a town like Bath and became a town like Brighton. At first sexes were segregated and bathed naked, as can be seen from some of the caricatures of Rowlandson, but the practice was less startling than it might seem because of the bathing machines which were provided with an umbrella-like awning. This made it possible to descend into the water without being seen.

Men long continued to bathe naked, but women began to be provided in the early years of Victoria's reign with a kind of ample poncho with a hole in the middle, or a large cloak tied round the neck. This spread out on the surface of the water to a considerable distance, leaving the limbs at liberty beneath. When the wearer emerged from the sea the cloak draped itself round her in ample folds.

Bathing costumes, properly so called, reached an extreme degree of elaboration in the 1870s and 1880s. A high-necked tunic with half-sleeves trimmed with lace concealed most of the body. The legs were clad in trousers similarly trimmed and extending to mid-calf. A strange feature was the practice of wearing a corset underneath. It seemed impossible to forgo the fashionable tight waist even in the water, and 'rustless' corsets were specially designed for the purpose.

There would have been no point in this when bathing from the old-fashioned 'machine' which was trundled into the water by a horse. But the French had invented the bathing chalet which made necessary a short walk down to the beach. English visitors, being presumably more modest than their Continental sisters, were advised to bathe only early in the morning, but most of the *belles baigneuses* were, of course, only too eager to display their finery and their figures. Many of them never entered the water at all.

Bathing costumes were no less fashionable and 'proper' in

146

'Le Minimum': regulation costu the Île de Levant in the 1960s.

the early years of the present century. It was even thought necessary to wear stockings, either black or white. It became the mode at this period for professional beauties and musical comedy actresses to have themselves photographed in bathing costumes for the illustrated papers. They pose, in front of the studio waves, in dresses which, except that they are a little shorter, might be the ordinary summer dresses of the day.

There was a constant tendency to follow the fashion of the hour. In 1919, for instance, the over-tunic of the bathing dress was short and wide like the prevailing mode, and high-laced boots were worn. Bathing caps were beginning to be worn but were not yet made of rubber and were obviously not meant to be immersed.

In 1920 the over-skirt shows the wide pannier effect of contemporary evening dresses, and in 1925 the shapelessness of the gowns of the period is reflected in the tubular bathing costumes. They are still, by modern standards, extremely ample; in fact in the 1920s the ridiculous position was reached that bathing costumes were almost more 'proper' than ordinary dresses. Women who wore the 'one-piece' bathing costume still sometimes faced prosecution.

What reduced bathing costumes to their present exiguous dimensions was not bathing, but *sun*-bathing. The backless bathing suit and the 'two-piece' with bare midriff were the progenitors of a host of evening gowns which would never have been designed as they were unless these particular sports costumes had set them an example.

Cycling costume, 1880.

Perhaps never before had civilized women bared their backs to the waist, and there was a moment in the '30s when women's evening dresses seemed to have been designed *to be seen from the back*. Perhaps they were—the dress of a modern ballroom dancer *is* seen from the back—but the form this peculiar décolletage took was decided by a sports costume.

The girl cyclist has already been mentioned. It is obvious that her present costume—when she is riding for pleasure, and therefore wearing it as a sports costume—has long passed the stage when it was capable of influencing current modes. However, when cycling began, it was a very different matter. For one thing it was, in the beginning, a high-class pursuit. There was no taint of work or utility about it. Indeed, the earliest lady cyclists in London used to drive down to Battersea Park

147

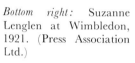
Top left: Tennis costume, 1952.

Top right: Cycling costume, 1952.

Bottom right: Suzanne Lenglen at Wimbledon, 1921. (Press Association Ltd.)

Bottom left: Cycling costume, 1894.

in a carriage, take the bicycle from the waiting groom, ride round the park and drive back in the carriage to luncheon. The clothes they wore were revolutionary: breeches or bloomers,[1] or, at the very least, the divided skirt. What the live horse had failed to accomplish was brought about by this new mechanical steed. Not only the upper part of the body but the lower part, too, was masculinized.

Bicycling bloomers never became ordinary wear, but the other masculine elements passed over into the tailor-made of the early twentieth century and then, as a tweed, became the regulation costume for shooting and other country pursuits. This also affected clothes for golf, although it was still quite correct, up to the First World War, to play golf in a blouse and skirt.

It may be said, therefore, that sports clothes have, in the past, exercised considerable influence on women's clothes, and that this influence reaches its maximum just before they stereotype themselves into specialized garments. From then on they tend towards utility, giving protection against the weather if they are intended for winter pastimes and tending to shrink to mere vestiges if used for summer sports. When they have so stereotyped themselves, their influence on ordinary dress is nil, except for oddities such as the backless evening gown.

The influence of sports clothes on men's wear continues and is likely to continue. Already young men are adopting what used to be sports costume—tweed coat and grey-flannel trousers—for ordinary wear. The new sports outfit seems likely to consist of corduroy trousers and some version of the battledress blouse or American lumber jacket. And so the whole cycle begins anew.

[1] There is some controversy on this point. Sir Basil Liddell Hart informed the present writer that he had *never* seen lady cyclists in bloomers at this period.

Skiing costume, 1910.

Skating costume, 1954.

Skating costume, 1905.

Skiing costume, 1954

Oh! Reform it Altogether!

12 Fashionable dress, that is dress which either proclaims the wearer's social status or provokes the attention of the opposite sex, or does both these things, has been the subject of attack from the beginning. It has been denounced on moral and religious grounds but, from the middle of the seventeenth century, there is a change of emphasis. The transition can be noted most clearly in France, where edicts of 1629 and 1633 forbade the use of lace and embroidery, whether manufactured at home or abroad. Further edicts of 1634 and 1644 prohibited the decoration of garments with gold or silver thread. In these prohibitions Cardinal Richelieu and Cardinal Mazarin were presumably still thinking in terms of the *wickedness* of luxury. But Colbert, a generation later, was thinking in terms of the national economy when he attempted to discourage the use of foreign materials. He wished to promote the native *industries de luxe*. This new attitude might be called economic Puritanism, and is still manifest from time to time in periods of financial stringency, as we shall see when we come to consider the efforts of Sir Stafford Cripps to control feminine fashions after World War II.

In the nineteenth century the attack on Fashion came from a different quarter, or rather, from two different quarters. It was denounced as anti-aesthetic and as anti-hygienic; and there was, indeed, something to be said on both counts. The beauty of the body, especially of the female body, resides in the harmony of its proportions; and this harmony it is precisely the function of Fashion to destroy.

A visitor from another planet, who judged women only by the shape of their clothes and had no clear notion of the human body underneath, might very well come to the conclusion that they belonged, down the ages, not to one race of creature but

150

to half a dozen species as different as the elephant and the giraffe. About the year 1600 the fashionable women of Western Europe appeared to have bodies divided into two halves. The lower half was the shape of a drum, and into this was inserted a wedge-shaped corsage terminating in a sharp point. Their heads appeared enormously enlarged and their shoulders also; they had no legs at all. A hundred years later women's hips were prodigiously wide when seen from the front but quite narrow when seen from the side. In the middle of the nineteenth century skirts were once more of gigantic proportions all the way round, even if the crinoline was somewhat more graceful than the old farthingale. When the crinoline was replaced by the bustle the emphasis was on the posterior and women appeared to be the shape of a camel whose hump had slipped from his back and come to rest on his hind quarters. In the early 1880s this hump had disappeared but the waist

Music title. Girls in costume advocated by Mrs Bloomer but not actually worn at this period (*c*. 1860).

was mercilessly pinched in until women looked like wasps. And all the time the notion that the female of the species had no legs was carefully cultivated.

In 1944 an exhibition, arranged by the Viennese architect Bernard Rudofsky, was put on at the Museum of Modern Art in New York, under the title 'Are Clothes Modern?'. The object was to show the similarity between many modern fashions and the modes of savages, and this the numerous examples made abundantly clear. But perhaps the most interesting exhibit consisted of four plaster figures 'executed by Constantine Nivola', and representing 'the female body as moulded by Fashion'. The woman of 1870 was shown as a centaur; the woman of 1904 had only one breast (the 'mono-bosom', which was strangely considered more moral than two breasts); the woman of 1913, the era of the hobble-skirt, had only one leg; and the woman of 1928 had no breasts and no posterior. We have attempted, in a previous chapter, to account for this strange shifting of emphasis; but it is, quite plainly, anti-aesthetic; and who more likely to take up the cudgels against it than the champions of the Aesthetic Movement?

In retrospect, it is easy to laugh at the Aesthetes, particularly if we see them through the eyes of George Du Maurier and W. S. Gilbert, and many of their antics were, no doubt, absurd enough. But they certainly had some justification for their protest, especially in the 1880s when a second bustle even uglier than the first had imposed itself upon the whole fashionable world. It is amusing to note, however, that this new bustle was not made of horsehair but of a kind of wire netting. It was advertised as the 'Hygienic Bustle: warranted to be less heating to the spine than any other'.

This was at least a concession to health, and was a sign that the Aesthetic protest was something more than a revolt against ugliness; in fact the Aesthetes, the medical men and the 'New Woman' were united in their opposition to the fashionable dress of the day. Early in 1887 a meeting was held at the Westminster Town Hall to launch the National Dress Society, the name of which was later transformed, by the change of a single letter, into the *Rational* Dress Society.

Mrs Oscar Wilde, wife of England's leading Aesthete, was in the chair, but the principal speaker was Viscountess Hambledon, a somewhat formidable example of the New

Woman, who cracked a riding whip to emphasize the points of her oration. But the points she made were rational enough. Her main protest was against the hampering nature and sheer *weight* of the clothes fashionable women were expected to wear; and, as they grew older, they were made to wear even heavier garments:

> The older a woman gets, the more unnecessary things it is considered proper for her to pile on her unfortunate person. Her very bonnet is heavier; her mantle and dress of heavier and richer material; her skirts longer and her *improver* [i.e. her bustle] larger. . . . The average weight of the dress of a grandmother among the richer classes was not less than 15lb.[1]

Skirts were so long and hampering that women were compelled to take very short steps, and it was impossible for them to walk upstairs without gathering up a considerable weight of material. Lady Hambledon, quoting the remark of a trade journal that 'there is no need for a woman to be able to do more than use her limbs in a feminine fashion', went on to claim that 'petticoats are exhausting, unhealthy, dirty and dangerous. The trouser is not only more comfortable, healthy and clean, but also more decent, as less liable to derangement'.

She herself was wearing 'Turkish trousers of black satin *merveilleux* with a sash round the hips, and a black velvet jacket trimmed with jet *passementerie*, caught together at the waist with a buckle over a full waistcoat of white satin and lace'. Perhaps it was a pity that a lady in her social position was not at hand in 1851 when Mrs Bloomer made her pioneer attempt to reform female dress. Her gallant effort had been killed by public ridicule, and by the fact that she made no converts among the upper classes. But a generation later the climate of opinion was already changing.

One of the main charges against fashionable dress was the tight-lacing which it involved. *All* the ladies on the platform with Lady Hambledon had discarded their corsets as a mark of their emancipation; and although the majority of women were not inclined to follow them there was a growing recognition of the dangers of an excessively slim waist. The very sensible Mrs Haweis remarks:

> We are not denying the necessity for some close fitting garment as a support to the body, and an improvement to the figure; people

[1] *The Pictorial World*, 1887.

153

who refuse to wear any corset at all look very slovenly: but we must protest against a machine that, pretending to be a servant, is, in fact, a tyrant. . . . Nothing is so ugly as a pinched waist; it puts the hips and shoulders invariably out of proportion in width, and it is a practice more culpable than the Chinese one of deforming the foot—in this case, no vital organ is interfered with, whilst in deforming the waist, almost all vital organs are affected by the pressure, and the ribs pushed out of their proper place. . . . What sensible man or woman can pity the fool who faints, perhaps in the midst of a dance or conversation, from the unbearable pressure on the heart, caused by stays or girdle—or, if they pity, do not also blush for her?

Such arguments would seem to have been unanswerable, but even the medical profession was divided, and some doctors defended tight-lacing on the ground that such support was necessary to the female figure. A writer in the *Englishwoman's Domestic Magazine* for 1868 remarks:

It is seldom that girls are allowed to attain the age of fourteen before commencing stays. The great secret is to begin their use as early as possible. There is no article of civilised dress which, when first begun to be worn, does not feel uncomfortable to those who have never worn it before. . . . Even the most extreme lacing can be employed without injury to health. . . . Very many of the strongest and healthiest women one sees in society habitually practise tight-lacing and apparently do so with impunity.

This is special pleading indeed, and one need hardly add that such opinions were totally unsupported by the facts. Other, more rational, voices were raised, and already in 1854 we find Mrs Merrifield, the once-famous authoress of *Dress as a Fine Art*, protesting: 'What a host of evils follows in the steps of tight-lacing; indigestion, hysteria, spinal curvature, liver complaints, disease of the heart, cancer, early death! These are a few of them, and enough to make both mothers and daughters tremble.' The great pioneer of female emancipation, Miss Ada S. Ballin, writing in 1885, remarks rather comically that: 'Tight-lacing must be banished from the mind and body of the woman who would ride the iron steed.' The 'iron steed' in question was, of course, the bicycle, or rather, when Miss Ballin wrote, the tricycle!

By the '90s the medical profession was almost unanimous, and then came the strange invention, the 'Health Corset'. This was a corset so boned as to be straight down the front, thus

154

pushing forward the bosom, thrusting back the hips, and so taking the pressure off the abdomen. This corset lasted throughout the Edwardian era and was responsible for the

Past and Present.

curiously typical S-shaped stance of the period. But Fashion defeated the doctors. The new 'Health Corset' was, in the end, laced so tightly that the effect was almost as deleterious as before. It is amazing that women in such a contrivance managed to survive at all, and still more amazing that some of them produced children.

It was not until the First World War that tight-lacing was really abandoned, and then not at all for health reasons, but because of the urge towards sexual emancipation which was characteristic of this period. And so Fashion accomplished what the doctors and the moralists combined had so conspicuously failed to do.

Meanwhile, what was happening to the would-be reformers of male dress? While his wife was supporting Lady Hambledon, Oscar Wilde was calling for a 'notable and joyous dress for men'. Certainly there was nothing very notable and joyous about the fashionable male costume of the 1880s, and Wilde's prophecy that 'the dress of the future . . . will use drapery to a great extent, and will abound with joyous colour' has found only a measure of fulfilment in the dress of the hippies and flower people.

The reform of men's dress remains an intractable problem. Just before World War II the B.B.C., experimenting with the new toy of television, staged at Alexandra Palace a meeting of male dress reformers, and the most striking thing about it was the poverty of invention displayed by the enthusiasts. One of them wore a costume not far removed from Fauntleroy's, one of them wore a version of eighteenth-century dress with ruffles and *rabat*, one of them was dressed as a monk and one of them as a Boy Scout! In our own day, such 'dress reform' as can be noted has merely followed what seems the inevitable process of bringing in a sports costume and gradually adapting it for ordinary wear. The only real advance has been in the weight of the materials used. Men wear less than they used to and that can perhaps be considered an advance.

World War II raised once more the question of economic Puritanism and even when the war was over dress materials were in short supply and clothes rationing was still in force. Hence the uproar in 1947 over the 'New Look'. Old-fashioned moralists would—or should—have been delighted with the advent of longer skirts; the new moralists were alarmed at the

'How Miss Kitty Loftus loo
Bloomers.' (From *The Sketch*, 18

prospect of more cloth being needed. We are reminded of how stringent clothes rationing was by the official announcement that 'Princess Elizabeth will be given 100 coupons for her wedding. Bridesmaids will get 23 coupons each, pages 10 coupons each.' There is something delightfully bone-headed and bureaucratic in those 23 coupons for bridesmaids. Was it a compromise between those on some official committee who wanted to be generous and allow 25 coupons and those who thought 20 should be enough?

That arch economic Puritan Sir Stafford Cripps, who was the President of the Board of Trade, did not approve of the 'New Look' at all. He maintained that in 'the economic battle for democracy' long skirts could have no place. And the formidable Mrs Braddock, rejecting it as 'the ridiculous whim of idle people', went on to claim that 'British women have not agitated for the long skirt. Their strong feeling is that things should be left as they are. Most women today are glad to have any clothes they can get hold of.'

It was all in vain. Mr Richard Crossman tells us what happened:

> That Mrs Braddock had misjudged her sex was demonstrated a few months later when M. Dior arrived in London to stage a sumptuous dress show at the Savoy Hotel. Next day the dresses were shown secretly to the Queen, Princess Margaret and the Duchess of Kent, at the French Embassy. This was a ceremony, Mr Phillips tells us, which the public and the press were not informed about. Not even the Queen's dressmaker, Norman Hartnell, knew that Princess Margaret had been converted to the New Look. By the 1948 Easter Parade, the New Look had conquered the West End. And on 17 March Princess Margaret wore it in public. On the same day, an almost unknown young politician who had succeeded Sir Stafford Cripps at the Board of Trade permitted a senior civil servant to declare 'we cannot dictate to women the length of their skirts.' The voice of wisdom was that of Harold Wilson.[1]

One possible, if drastic, solution of all the problems of clothing the human body was offered by the nudists or, as they preferred to call themselves, the Naturists. What could be more natural than wearing no clothes at all? Yet even this was denied by Eric Gill, who brought out a book designed 'to show that

[1] R. H. S. Crossman, reviewing in the *New Statesman*, 18 October 1963, Michael Sissons' and Philip French's *The Age of Austerity*. 1963.

man is, by nature, a clothed animal and that, far from being a naked animal who puts clothes on, he is a clothed animal who takes them off'.[1] This quaint notion seems to have been derived from a belief in the 'natural law' as expounded by St Thomas Aquinas, but Gill's own ideas on the subject are more than a little confused. It was to be expected that he should attack capitalism and contraception: but he also attacks Puritanism as incompatible with Christianity. If he had studied the Early Fathers with the same attention as he had given to the writings of Belloc and Chesterton, he might have come to a very different conclusion. He exalts the beauty of the naked human body, a theme which would not have found much acceptance in the first two centuries of our era. But he was surely justified in thinking that the monk's robes he habitually wore (as a member of the Third Order of St Francis) were more comfortable and 'sensible' than the close-fitting tailor-made costume of his male contemporaries. And his claim too that 'man's primary need in clothes is vestments and robes' contains at least a grain of truth.

The Naturists, too, exalted the beauty of the naked human body, but their main object was a moral and social one. They claimed, with justice, that in a nudist camp class-consciousness was impossible, and they denied, also justly, that nudism excited eroticism except in the Peeping Toms outside. Similar notions seem to have inspired a whole series of movements as a protest against that hatred of the body inculcated by Christian asceticism. A sect of Adamites is heard of as early as the second century but they left no records of their own and we only know of them and of their 'aberrations and excesses' from St Augustine, St Epiphanius and other bitter opponents. They claimed, we are told, to have recovered the primal innocence, wore no clothes when they assembled for worship, and called their church Paradise.

What happened to the early Adamites is not known. They were certainly persecuted and disappeared from history for a thousand years. Then they were suddenly heard of again in the Netherlands under the name of Brethren and Sisters of the Free Spirit. They were suppressed with fire and sword, but reappeared in the fourteenth century. They were called Beghards and later Picards, which seems to imply an origin in

[1] Eric Gill. *Clothes*. 1931.

158

Example of a new style for men (1968)
by Morris Gay Ltd of Toronto (photograph by Gerald Campbell).

the Low Countries and what is now the north of France. They were sufficiently powerful, in Bohemia, to take possession of an island in the river Nezarka (an island is an excellent place for a nudist colony, as some modern enthusiasts have found) and to defend themselves for a time against their enemies. On their island, it is said, they 'gave themselves up to a shameful communism'—whatever that may mean.

However, the Island Paradise was not destined to survive, for in 1421 the fanatical Hussite leader, Ziska, almost exterminated them and the survivors were scattered. It was not until 1781 that the same, or a similar cult, was revived in Bohemia, owing to the Edict of Toleration issued by the enlightened Emperor Joseph II, and the Neo-Adamites managed to last for nearly seventy years. They were suppressed by force in 1849, the nineteenth century thereby showing itself less tolerant than the eighteenth.

In all these movements there was a fanatical religious element which now only survives among the Doukhobors, an anarchistic sect banished from Russia to Asiatic Georgia and finding a refuge in Western Canada in 1898. There are now fifteen thousand of them and they give much trouble to the authorities by refusing, among other things, to send their children to school. They do not go about naked all the time, but organize nude marches of protest which occasionally land them in jail. But their survival is threatened not so much by the Law as by the natural desire of the younger generation to escape from a rural and ascetic existence to the bright lights of the cities. The sect, as such, seems doomed to extinction.

What might be called secular nudism, on the other hand, has shown a startling expansion in the last half century. Beginning in Germany before the advent of Hitler, the cult spread rapidly all over Europe. At the present day it is estimated that a quarter of a million Germans practise nudism with the approval, or at least with the permission, of the authorities. There are even public nudist beaches, notably that at Abersiwien, on the island of Sylt, near the Danish-German frontier. France has its famous Île de Levant, near Toulon. In England there are said to be fifty clubs catering for ten thousand nudists; and in America there are approximately thirty thousand registered nudists. There are even Naturist conventions, sun-bathing queens and nudist marriages. Sometimes there is trouble with the local authorities, but the United States courts have, on the whole, upheld private nudist camps and nudist magazines. Those who have visited such camps have been unanimous in their verdict that they are well conducted and give no cause for scandal of any kind. So we arrive at the paradoxical conclusion that the only way in which we can be cleansed of the Pride of Life and (almost) cleansed of the Lust of the Eye, is to wear no clothes at all.

Male and Femal
Created He Ther

13 The study of Fashion, of the clothes men and women have worn at different epochs of history, was until recently considered by many to be a somewhat superficial pursuit, a kind of elegant trifling, at best a very humble footnote to the record of political events, religious movements and economic trends. That Louis XIV wore a periwig or the Empress Eugénie a crinoline seemed to serious historians a matter scarcely worth mentioning, certainly not worth dwelling on. Such things were merely the 'follies of Fashion' and therefore meaningless. The follies of Fashion! Even the Puritans, in their most acrid denunciations of the extravagance of dress, did not fall into this superficiality. They were much nearer the mark when they described Fashion not as foolish, but as wicked. It was at least an acknowledgement that the clothes people wear have a meaning, even if moralists have consistently disapproved of what that meaning was.

It is of course quite possible to spend a lifetime merely listing Fashion's vagaries, as they are called, and this many writers on the subject have been content to do. The result is a jungle through which the most determined traveller can hardly hack his way. Bustles came in in 1870; hats were very large in 1911; in 1925 women cut off their hair. It is all very difficult to remember and even more difficult to understand. But, in recent years (it is surprising how recent), there has been a growing number of writers who have concerned themselves not only with the 'What' of Fashion, but with the 'When' and the 'How', and some have even ventured into the difficult question of the 'Why'.

This 'Why' is a delusive sprite indeed, a veritable Jack o' Lantern, leading the traveller through the political woods, across the economic deserts, over the mountain peaks of

162

religion and, even at last, into the morasses of psycho-analysis. He who would make this journey must have an unsleeping eye and indefatigable patience and he must be well provided with talismans, for he meets magic at every turn. Yet his reward is great for, as he persists, he finds that this world of human habiliments is not a chaos, that tracks lead into one another and broaden into roads and avenues, and that the meaning of something very small is sometimes the meaning of something very big.

Male and female costume, 1860. ('They might belong to different species . . .')

Modesty in Dress

One of the first attempts to plumb the deeper meanings of Fashion was Carlyle's *Sartar Resartus*. Diogenes Teufelsdröckh, Professor-of-Things-in-General (under which grotesque mask Carlyle himself was hiding) had evolved a philosophy of clothes which, he contended, was, if rightly understood, the key to the Universe. He had even written a vast Germanic tome on the subject, of which we are given the quite imaginary title: *Die Kleider, ihr Werden und Wirken* (Clothes, their Origin and Influence). *Weissnichtvo*, 1831. But such glimpses of the contents as we are allowed do not, unfortunately, throw much light on the subject. The fantasy of a naked House of Lords is no more than an excuse for a meditation on Man's place in the Universe, and the chapter on Dandyism (the strange phenomenon to which Baudelaire was later to bring so penetrating an intelligence) is merely an excuse to emphasize the scandalous difference between the luxury of a Brummell and the abject poverty of an Irish peasant.

Carlyle was, of course, too early to be even aware of psychology and anthropology, and even if he knew of, he was certainly not converted to, the economic interpretation of history. This theory, once it had been absorbed, certainly proved capable of forcing many locks, and to some it seemed the only key needed for the purpose. This was certainly true of Thorsten Veblen, whose revolutionary *Theory of the Leisure Class* has been so often referred to in the foregoing pages.

But it does not offer anything like a complete explanation. The Utility Principle does operate in dress (even if it sometimes operates in reverse) but it is not the only principle involved. If it were, we should all wear dungarees for the greater part of the day, and soldiers' uniforms would not always be one war behind. It is not even the most powerful influence at work. The Hierarchical Principle (as regards men) and the Seduction Principle (as regards women) have much more to say in the matter. The one makes men attractive to women by suggesting that they enjoy a sufficiently high social status to ensure the prosperity of the brood, the other makes women attractive to men by a frank exploitation of the allurements of sex. Clothes have therefore (at least in part) a sexual meaning, and we are already leaving the world of Marx and entering the world of Freud.

It is only below the poverty line that the Utility Principle is

164

A Renaissance page anticipating mini-skirt.

the dominant one. People below this line obviously do not wear what they like, but what they can get. Even then the clothes they wear are not the most useful clothes (except for the elementary purpose of keeping warm) but simply the discarded clothes of more fortunate classes, and these were only to a very limited degree constructed on principles of utility.

When people are free to buy what clothes they like, what do they buy? On the economic interpretation it would seem that the more control of purchasing power they had the more gorgeous they would be. The more liberty, the more frills, brighter colours, more fantasy in hats. Surely the fall of a tyrant is a feather in the cap of the ordinary man. Why doesn't he wear it?

In spite of sumptuary laws, passed and re-passed and always disregarded, under a king (by which is meant a real king, not a constitutional monarch), men's clothes are gorgeous. Under a democracy they are plain to the point of drabness. There were plumed hats in plenty at the Court of Louis XIV but none at the Court of Louis-Philippe.

Sensible men, it will be objected, do not like fine clothes. Men conscious of their own dignity are content with a noble simplicity. Both statements beg far too many questions, and evade too many definitions. Is a top-hat noble? Perhaps. It is certainly not simple and nobody could call it an object of utility. And surely liberty is worth rejoicing over. Why are all these free men dressed as for a funeral? Are they, by any chance, in mourning for the king they have deposed?

Women are an even stranger case. Even 'sensible' women are allowed to take some pleasure in fine clothes. Surely when women are free, when they are emancipated, both politically and economically, when they have money of their own to spend as they choose, surely they will exploit their feminine charms to the utmost, revel in silks and satins and brocades, pile up their 'crowning glory' into a very monument of triumph and, most of all, reflect in the brightness of their chosen colours the gaiety of their hearts.

Alas! emancipated woman does none of these things. In fact she does the precise opposite. She throws away the rich and patterned stuffs, and her corset with them, she makes the lines of her garments as straight as Nature will allow, and sometimes straighter, she discards her jewellery, she cuts off her

165

hair. If she intended to go into a convent forthwith she could hardly behave differently. Most striking of all, she eschews all bright colours and wears white (as in the period following the French Revolution), beige (as in the decade following the First World War) or some other pale shade, as she is almost certain to do in the era of complete emancipation which is just beginning.

There is surely something here which needs a little explanation, unless we throw in our hand altogether as investigators of the 'Why', and content ourselves with recording a series of arbitrary and unrelated facts. The impulse to dress in a certain way springs from the very deepest level of the psyche, and if this is so we must accept the universally symbolic nature of clothes. Clothes—all clothes—are symbolic of something. But symbolic of what?

The old-fashioned psychologists had no light to throw on this subject. They moved their counters—labelled Will, Fancy, Imagination, Memory and the like—over a chequer board of their own devising and the game had, no doubt, a certain intellectual interest. But a game it was, and it threw about as much light upon the problems of the human soul as a game of chess might throw upon the campaigns of Napoleon. About as much, but certainly no more. The psycho-analysts are sometimes accused of arbitrariness, but their arbitrariness was nothing to this; and, if they have done nothing else, they have at least reminded us that the forces which control the psyche are not half black and half white and that they are capable of moving in more than two dimensions. Have they any light to throw on this subject?

On the whole, the psycho-analysts have given but scant attention to the study of clothes, and there is obviously a field here for some startling discoveries if the right brains could be brought to bear upon the subject. But some of them have thrown out hints which may help to give us at least a signpost or a clue, and two of them in particular (curiously enough, they are both Hungarians) have developed theories which seem to have considerable bearing on the question before us.

Ferenczi, in his *Versuch einer Genitaltheorie*, certainly pushes the study of the libido as far back as it will go, and Géza Róheim, in his *Animism, Magic and the Divine King*, has developed Ferenczi's theories further and sought to apply them to

166

anthropological problems. Ferenczi takes as his starting point the most primitive form of living creature. In such a creature there is, of course, no differentiation of organs. It is at one moment all mouth, at another all stomach; it propagates its kind by fission, by simply dividing in two, and in the act of parturition is, therefore, at the same instant, all mother and all child.

Advance from such a blob of jelly can only come in one way: by specialization, by differentiating the various functions even of the most primitive life and assigning them to different parts of the organism. In the original cells which contained life there must have been a tension when fission was about to take place: a tendency to divide and a tendency to resist division. 'In animals with more specialized functions and organs we have the ejection of gametic cells as a substitute for fission.' This means that there is one part of the organism which specializes in housing (and, as occasion arises, ejecting) the gametic cells; that is, there is a sexual organ. And by the concentration of libidinal impulses in the genitals (however rudimentary these may be) the rest of the organism escapes from the libidinal tension and is free to devote itself to other matters. 'The penis', Ferenczi tells us, 'is the instrument that relieves the organs of the body of the superfluous libido and thus makes it possible for them to adapt themselves to reality.' Or, in the words of Róheim, 'the erotic reality-principle, that is, the attainment of genital primacy is closely connected with, and is the condition of the attainment of, the general reality-principle'.

If, however, for any reason, genital-primacy is lost (e.g. by castration), then the whole organism is re-eroticized. There can therefore be a flux and a reflux of the libido. Its concentration Ferenczi calls the genitopetal tendency, and its diffusion he calls the genitofugal tendency. And this idea of the libido flux which we owe to the Hungarian savant is most suggestive. It throws, for example, a beam of light upon the reason for the *diffused* eroticism of the female body as opposed to the genital primacy of the male. But we will leave this question for the moment while we follow Róheim in his application of the theory to questions of social anthropology. For what is true of the individual in this matter is true also of the community. If the primitive community is to adapt itself to reality

167

and therefore be efficient in securing survival, it must concentrate its libido, it must grow itself a penis. This symbolic penis is the Jealous Sire of the Primal Horde.

Freud's theory of the Primal Horde was bitterly attacked even by some eminent anthropologists and it would be impossible in the present study even to summarize the controversies that have raged around it. But there does seem to have been a stage in human history when the Old Man of the group had all the pleasure and procreation for himself, until the day came when he was deposed by a younger and stronger man. So matters long continued as they continue to this day in, for example, herds of deer. But humanity escaped from this stage into another, a condition of affairs which is usually known as Totemism.

Totemism is a very mysterious and complicated thing, but of its wide extension and of its persistence among certain peoples to this day there can be no doubt. It seems to have arisen by a concerted revolt of the young men of the tribe against the Old Man of the tribe, and it resulted, not in his mere replacement by another, but in his permanent deposition. The tribe has now no Father, alive and active. Instead it has a mythical ancestor and this ancestor has usually an animal form. What has taken place, to use Ferenczi's language, is a sudden reflux of the libido from the penis to the body (that is, a reflux from the personified penis to the body politic), accompanied by the self-castration of society, the autochthony of the penis.

> This phrase in social development [he says] may be regarded as a parallel to hysteria. In this disease we find a re-genitalization of the auto-erotic zones, in savage society a gerontocratic rule, a tribe with many fathers or phalli. The animal phobia is a typical feature of infantile hysteria, an attempt to project the embodiment of the libido outside the organism, to have an imaginary non-human penis. In society this form of settling difficulties is represented by totemism, a society of equals with a mythical father equivalent. However, the main characteristics of totemic society are repression and anxiety. The strain of repression becomes too great and in the course of evolution society again grew a penis, the king.[1]

Now it is generally accepted, even by those who are not psycho-analysts and would, no doubt, be shocked by the

[1] Quoted by Róheim, *op. cit.* page 309.

psycho-analytical approach to the subject, that the advent of kings coincides with the rise of agriculture. In Róheim's words: 'only people acquainted with the elements of agriculture have Divine Kings. . . . Agriculture means incest with Mother Earth.' We may certainly agree that primitive kings were agriculturalists, and traces of their function remain to this day. 'Among the Ho a good king is a good farmer, and ploughing is the chief ceremonial duty of the Chinese emperor.'

The Divine King is responsible for the fertility of the whole tribe, or, as it has now become, the whole realm, not in the actual, physical sense of the Jealous Sire but in a metaphorical, or rather, a magical sense. He is regarded as not only the symbol but the instrument of fertility. By sympathetic magic, by a Holy Marriage, he promotes crops and herds, and the whole life of the community; and so important is this function of his that when his strength begins to fail he is, at least in the early stages of kingship, killed and replaced.

The Divine King is the personified penis of the whole community and it is for this reason that, as has often been noted, all his insignia and all his ceremonies are phallic. Phallic is his sceptre, phallic is his crown; his insertion of his head into the circlet at his coronation is a symbolic coitus. The oil of his anointing, the water of his lustrations, the cross embroidered on his robe or carried in his hand: all these are symbols of his function, the magical apparatus with which he goes to work. He is the source of all life, by him the people prosper. He also bears their sins, for he is the projection of their own libido, and 'this is just what the original rulers were made for, as realizations of, and scapegoats for, the unconscious desires of their subjects'.[1]

Perhaps this explains the curious fact that the *popular* kings of history have always been the notorious lechers. A 'good' king (using good as the moralists use it) is simply a king who is not doing his job. It is the business of a king to be the personified phallus of the whole community, and personified phalli can hardly be expected to be celibate in any sense of the word.

> In pious times, ere priestcraft did begin,
> Before polygamy was made a sin;
> When man on many multiplied his kind,

[1] Róheim, *op. cit.*, page 225.

Nor one to one was cursedly confined;
When nature prompted, and no law denied
Promiscuous use of concubine and bride;
Then Israel's monarch after Heaven's own heart,
His vigorous warmth did variously impart
To wives and slaves; and wide as his command,
Scatter'd his Maker's image through the land.

There is nothing to quarrel with in Dryden's famous lines except in the phrase 'ere priestcraft did begin'. For if the Divine King was a king in the completest sense of the word, he was also a priest, and even his shadows today, at their coronation, assume the ecclesiastical as well as the royal vestments.

Let us, however, return to Ferenczi's doctrine of the libido-flux. With the establishment of divine kingship, the individual subjects have now got rid of the concentration of the libido in themselves by projecting it upon another. In them, therefore, the flow becomes genitofugal; that is, there is a genitalization, an eroticizing of all the rest of the body. The whole of the individual male body is once more charged with libido. It has become *lovable*, and this love of the body expresses itself in fine clothes. This is to advance beyond the position taken up by either Ferenczi or Róheim, but it seems to follow logically from their argument.

The existence of a Divine King means the wearing of gorgeous clothes by all those men (we are still dealing only with men) who live above the poverty line; in particular, of course, by the courtiers. Henceforward it is the Court which establishes the standard of dress and inaugurates new fashions. It is obvious that the courtiers of Xerxes were more gorgeous than the citizens of Athens. When Julius Caesar first appeared at the Court of Cleopatra it is unlikely that he outshone the Queen's attendants. But, in the second generation of Caesars, that public official, the Imperator, proclaimed himself divine, and the way was clear from the simple white togas of the ancient Senate to all the vestments of Byzantium; and this gorgeousness lasted as long as the Empire endured.

From this point of view Christianity was a kind of new Totemism, transferring the Father of Mankind to the World of the Beyond. Its expression on earth was feudalism, which is Totemism in real earnest, even to the figurative animals which began to appear on knightly shields. There is a very rewarding

170

field of inquiry here for someone with the necessary technical knowledge. It is sufficient to note for the moment that the decay of heraldry (for it continued into the Renaissance period only as a parlour-game) coincides with the rise of absolute monarchies in the sixteenth century.

The new absolute monarchs could not quite call themselves Divine Kings, for a nominal Christianity still glossed their ambitions; but they did the next best thing. They called themselves Kings by Divine Right. It is a lawyer's, or a theologian's, quibble. It does not affect the point at issue. They still acted as personified phalli, and so induced in their subjects that genitofugal flux which enabled them to wear gorgeous clothes. If we take any dress, the aspect of which has been preserved for us in contemporary paintings and engravings, and try to deduce from it the degree of divinity which hedged the monarch whose subject the wearer of the costume was, the test seems to work.

It is important to note that dictators won't do. It is the divinity (the divine right) that matters, and the only way in which dictators can acquire divine right is by assuming the whole regalia, by making use of the magical apparatus. This, Napoleon almost succeeded in doing; this, Cromwell completely failed to do. And that is why English clothes are plain in the 1650s, when they were extremely gorgeous in France under *le Roi Soleil*.

With the return of Charles II, English Fashion flowered again, faltered once more under James II (was not his Divine Right the whole point at issue?) and took a definite plunge into the dark and the drab under William III. William, of course, did not believe in his own Divine Right. He was even at pains to protest against such a relic of divinity as touching for the King's Evil. He ventured to hope that God would cure his subjects' diseases and send them better sense. Naturally enough his touch failed to cure. 'Sense' (in *that* sense) has not much value as a therapeutic technique.

A constitutional monarch, whatever his personal prestige, can never be a personified phallus, or induce any of its results. That is why there is so striking a contrast between English clothes under George I and George II and French clothes under Louis XV. There is no lack of documentation. A thousand examples could be collected without difficulty. Louis XV

171

was a Divine King; he had *all* the attributes. There was no trace of divinity in the early Hanoverians, in spite of their regrettable morals.

When, after the death of Louis *le Bien-Aimé*, Frenchmen's clothes grew noticeably plainer, what does this mean except that, with Louis XVI, a change had come over the Monarchy? The divinity was plainly running out of the heels of its boots. With its final disappearance the transformation in dress becomes startling. It is the most drastic, and the most sudden, revolution in the whole history of Fashion. Frenchmen adopted English *country clothes*.

Napoleon's kingship was so obviously dependent upon his military victories, even when he *had* assumed a crown, that it is not surprising that male gorgeousness under him should chiefly express itself in military uniforms. Male civil dress did not recover its embroidered coat or its *talon rouge*. Nor did this happen under Louis XVIII, for not all the fervours of the *Ultras* could convince that portly sceptic that he was divine. Charles X almost succeeded in persuading himself, and so did our own George IV. Perhaps it is no accident that their reigns coincide with the rise of dandyism. But both kings disappeared in 1830, and what little colour remained in male costume can almost be caught in the act of fading away. Neither Louis-Philippe, nor our own Prince Consort, was in the least likely to revive it.

If we accept the view that the disappearance of the Divine King is equivalent to the castration of the community, then it follows that the genitofugal tendency immediately sets in and the whole body politic is once more genitalized. We enter a new period of neurosis (is it extravagant to equate this with the movement known as Romanticism?)[1] which neurosis is only prevented from being completely disruptive by the emergence of a new Totemism.

Totemism is essentially a race-consciousness expressing itself in the worship of the ancestors, the founders of the race. Its modern version is Nationalism, and it is very strange to see in this connection the emergence of the old animal symbols.

One has only to glance at the political cartoons of the second half of the nineteenth century to see this animal symbolism in

---

[1] For the neurotic character of Romanticism, see *The Romantic Agony* by Mario Praz, translated by Angus Davidson, 1933.

full blast. The Russian Bear, the *Coq Gaulois*, the British Lion. A visitor from Mars, looking through the files of *Punch*, for the period from the Crimean War to 1900, might well come to the conclusion that there was no essential difference between the beliefs of the modern European nations and those of the most primitive Australian tribes.

Totemism is essentially a defence-mechanism against the disintegration of the collective psyche. When it breaks down, without finding an effective substitute, as it has done in our own time, the burden of the libido becomes intolerable and the result is no longer merely a neurosis but a psychosis. In other words, the world goes mad, and in spite of all the good intentions of the conscious intelligence, and the pious platitudes of the moral sense, the Collective Unconscious begins to indulge in an orgy of destruction, ranging from such comparatively mild symptoms of insanity as burning coffee to homicide on a colossal scale. Will anyone have the courage, after what we have witnessed in our own lifetime, to call this an exaggerated picture? Is anyone still so superficial as to imagine that the fundamentals of politics are to be sought on the plane of the Conscious Intelligence? Mankind today is a dangerous lunatic confined, unfortunately, in an insufficiently padded cell.

So far we have only dealt with *men*, but the theory, with suitable modifications, can be applied to women. For the greater part of their history (certainly for almost the whole of recorded history), their situation has been not a relationship to the State but a relationship to a man. As the subject is to the king, so is the woman to her husband. He is her Divine King—or he isn't; and in both cases we find that the law we have discovered operates.

It cannot be too often stated that there is a fundamental difference between male and female costume. The one follows the Hierarchical Principle; the other the Seduction Principle. In other words, a man's clothes are a function of his relation to society; a woman's clothes are a function of her relation to man. That is, they are so until she is emancipated and, as the saying goes, 'enters politics'.

It is only comparatively recently that this problem has arisen at all and we have therefore to face the question why women have 'entered politics' so late. We may, I think, dismiss at once the view of sentimental feminists that this is due to an 'injustice', a denial of 'rights', a conspiracy on the part of men to keep women out of their proper place in society. There must be a deeper reason, and it lies in the nature of woman herself.

Ferenczi's view is that the concentration of the libido (in physical terms, the growth of a penis) is the condition for attaining what he calls sexual primacy, which is itself the basis for the integration of the personality. This integration, this sexual primacy, woman never attains; it is this that makes her a woman. Her whole body is, therefore, to varying degrees, genitalized or eroticized. But the mind seems unable to bear an overall distribution of the libido and since women are unable to concentrate it in one spot, they are compelled to be perpetually shifting the emphasis from one part to another, and this shifting of emphasis (Professor Flügel's 'shifting erogenous zone') is the basis of Fashion. That is why the word Fashion is properly applied only to women. There are various male costumes; there are no male 'fashions'. The fundamental principle is different.

Fashion is a function of the Seduction Principle with its need of perpetual novelty and change. Male costume is a function of the Hierarchical Principle, with its tendency to stereotype and even to formalize itself. The Seduction Principle might be called the Principle of Life; the Hierarchical Principle the Principle of Death. Or we can say that the Hierarchical Principle is the World and the Seduction Principle the Flesh.

As the man is to the State, so is the woman to the man. As the subject is to the king, so is the wife to the husband; but these 'truths' have only an historical, and therefore partial, validity. They are true within the framework of the Patriarchal System. That system is as old as history, but not very much older. Indeed it was its emergence that made 'history' possible; but in its early days, and for long afterwards, it preserved in its structure some relics of an earlier state of things, of mother-kin and mother-right. Certainly matriarchies have existed, even if the details of their organization are in dispute, and to them we all, subconsciously, long to return. They are the Garden of Eden, the Paradise of the Collective Psyche. And in such a paradise nothing, of course, is more natural than nudity.

There has been so much dispute as to the right meaning of

174

See-through mini-skirt by Gernreich. (Photograph by W Claxton.)

the terms patriarchal and matriarchal that some anthropologists prefer to discard them and to substitute patrilocal and matrilocal; for the important question is: *in whose house does the woman live?* For many thousands of years, in many primitive communities, a family consisted not of a man and his wife and their children, living in his house, but of a woman and her children living in her brother's house. The actual father of the children was a nocturnal visitor from another tribe—and not always the same man.

Such a state of affairs is so foreign to all those notions which we have inherited from the long ages of patriarchy, that it is only quite recently that people have begun to admit that any other system has, or could have, existed.

> Psychologists, ethnographers, and historians have hitherto regarded the relationships of power between the sexes exclusively from the outlook of masculine dominance. . . . Monosexual dominance . . . is always characterised by the spread of a tradition that the hegemony of the sex actually in power is eternal and unalterable. All the historical vestiges that conflict with this tradition are deliberately or unconsciously expunged from the record. Sometimes they are glossed over or falsified; sometimes they are erased; sometimes they are ignored. The inclination to get rid of the evidence somehow or other is stronger in proportion as the monosexual dominance is more absolute.[1]

And the Vaertings, from whom the above quotation is taken, go on to give some extraordinary examples.

There is, for instance, the plain statement of Diodorus Siculus that the marriage laws of the pre-Ptolemaic era in Egypt strongly favoured the women, in so much that women alone had the right to divorce a sexual partner, and could do so on payment of an indemnity and the refund of half the dowry which the husband had brought into the marriage. Even when this was confirmed by the discovery of papyri, Egyptologists refused to accept it. Indeed, any remark by an ancient writer which conflicted with the modern scholars' prejudices was somehow explained away. Max Müller, commenting on the passage in Herodotus in which he states that the Egyptian women left their homes on business while the men did the housework, decides that the Greek historian must have been speaking ironically. Man *must* have been dominant for such

[1] Mathilde and Mathias Vaerting. *The Dominant Sex.* Translated from German by Eden and Cedar Paul. 1923.

was a Law of Nature, and, by the same token, the primal family *must* have consisted of a man and his wife and their children. All polygamies, polyandries, group marriages and all other sexual customs which departed from this norm were perversions and degenerations, and, if found by missionaries in primitive societies still existing, must be firmly corrected.

Such a view was, of course, strongly reinforced by the acceptance of the literal truth of the Genesis story, and by the whole weight of a religion which was itself a projection of the patriarchal system. Sir Henry Maine based himself on Biblical examples when he asserted in his *Primitive Law*, published in 1851, that the patriarchal family was the original unit of society, larger units having been built up by the aggregation of such families into clan and tribe.

To most people all this seemed obvious enough, but other scholars did not share Maine's opinion and, shortly after the publication of *Primitive Law*, the Swiss jurist J. J. Bachofen brought out his *Das Mutterrecht*, in which he asserted that the primal state had been one of sexual promiscuity from which matriarchies had gradually emerged, to be replaced in their turn by patriarchies.

This view found little favour with the orthodox, even although they were as yet unaware of the bombshell which Darwin was about to explode under their feet; but those who were building up the new science of anthropology began to accumulate a mass of evidence which seemed to support Bachofen's opinion, and by the end of the century it is probable that most working anthropologists shared it.

The counter-blast was the work of the Finnish professor E. Westermarck, whose massive *History of Human Marriage* attempted to return to the position of Maine and to show that the patriarchal monogamous family was part of the Natural Law. The Natural Law is a concept very dear and useful to theologians, and Westermarck's book was received with acclamation. He was regarded as having restored the dignity of the father and the sanctity of family life.

Unfortunately Westermarck, as Gordon Rattray Taylor sarcastically remarks, 'was a man without anthropological qualifications' and his general thesis was soon recognized by scholars, if not by the general public, as wholly untenable. Robert Briffault's great work *The Mothers* provides a mass of

176

evidence to the contrary, and although Briffault certainly overstated his *own* case, it is fair to say that he completely demolished Westermarck's.[1]

Once established, the Patriarchal System, although somewhat modified in the later years of the Roman Empire and, in certain special cases, modified again under feudalism, remained substantially intact until about a hundred years ago. When at that period the Honourable Mrs Norton left her spendthrift and rascally husband he was still able to claim her earnings as an authoress, and to deprive her of the very means by which she was striving to keep herself and bring up her children. This was so obviously unjust that reform was inevitable, and, in England, after many struggles, there came into being what is known as the Married Woman's Property Act. This was the first nail in the coffin of male supremacy, the beginning of the collapse of the Patriarchal System.

For the Patriarchal System, like all human institutions, depends, ultimately, on a *sanction*. It depends on the husband being able to say: 'Leave my house, faithless woman.' If all he can say is: 'I will now leave your house, faithless woman,' the game is up. We have all known respectable families in England, and even more in America, which consisted of a woman and her children by successive husbands; and her present husband (the charming host who 'fixes' you a drink) may not be the father of any of them, and, when you call again may have been replaced by someone else.

There is no longer any social stigma attached to having children by successive husbands; but the formality of divorce and re-marriage is obviously only a transitional stage. When children are looked after by the State from birth to adult life, the function of the father dwindles to a single physical act; and successive physical acts can be performed by different men. This is Matriarchy in which no man knows which children of the tribe are his. We may not be there yet, but we are certainly going that way.

Few people—women least of all—realize the magnitude of this revolution. As the conserving element in human life, women are naturally conservative. They are, or think they

[1] Robert Briffault's *The Mothers* first appeared in 3 volumes in 1927. It is immensely long and detailed and the student is advised to read it in the one-volume edition, 'Abridged, with an Introduction by Gordon Rattray Taylor', published by Allen & Unwin in 1959.

are, the main defenders of the Family as it has so long been understood, the main supporters of Religion as it has been traditionally handed down. They see themselves as the champions of the freedom of the individual and of private property. They do not see that private property is itself a function of the patriarchal system; it means private property in women or it means nothing. Adultery was of no more a danger to the *institution* of the family than burglary is to the institution of private property, but the complete emancipation of women means the disappearance of the Family, unless by Family is meant merely the dam and her young. It also means the disappearance of those religions whose deities are projections of the patriarchal organization of society. Nothing is more pathetic than the spectacle of certain 'advanced' clergymen who think they can go on undermining the Patriarchal System (which they identify with the Capitalist System) and yet preserve intact the Patriarchal family, Patriarchal morals and the Patriarchal gods. These things stand—or fall—together.

If we accept this we cannot be as surprised as many people seem to be by the moral laxity of the present age. Patriarchies are repressive; Matriarchies are permissive. And, after all, a good deal of what is called the moral code was simply a set of rules for preserving the patriarch's property. He protected his daughters because a girl who had lost her virginity was not as valuable in the marriage market as one who had not. He watched jealously over his wife's chastity because he did not want to pay for bringing up children who might not be his own. It is true that he was much less concerned about his sons; indeed he sometimes encouraged their sexual adventures, so long as these adventures did not take place with girls of their own class. This was the origin of the 'double standard' so vehemently denounced by moralists and reformers of both sexes. The double standard has indeed been abolished, but not quite in the way these well-meaning people intended.

Women are now 'emancipated' and, probably for the first time in their history, *irreversibly* emancipated. Former waves of emancipation have always fallen back, generally through the rise of a new social class in which women were not yet emancipated. We have noted in a previous chapter that a wave of emancipation (which usually happens in a 'post-crisis

178

epoch') has a considerable effect on the clothes women wear. It straightens the lines, takes out the colour and ceases to emphasize the waist; in a word, it decreases the 'femininity' of female costume, it brings it nearer to male attire. A hundred years ago the clothes worn by the two sexes were sharply differentiated. Nothing could be more unlike, in materials, in silhouette and in general appearance than the costume of mid-Victorian man, in his frock coat and top-hat, and the crinoline of mid-Victorian woman.

This indeed was regarded as a moral necessity. Women like George Sand who adapted masculine attire, women like Mrs Bloomer who tried to introduce a very modest pair of pantaloons beneath quite a long skirt, were regarded as social outcasts. Men who wore what were regarded as effeminate clothes were similarly frowned upon; and in this the moralists of the day were simply carrying on a tradition at least as old as Christianity, which always taught that for men and women to wear clothes which resembled one another in any degree was a grave sin.

Today in Western Europe and America, but most noticeably perhaps in England, it is possible to walk behind two young people, each of them clad in tight jeans and loose sweater and each with long hair, and not know whether they are two girls, two boys, or one of each. The women have taken over the whole male outfit including the trousers, and it is precisely this which former generations would have found so shocking. Trousers! Perhaps no garment has ever had to bear so large a burden of ambivalence and repressed sexual guilt. For centuries people shied away from the very name of the thing. Even the eighteenth century, which we think of as an uninhibited and outspoken period, referred to breeches as 'small-clothes'. The nineteenth century admitted its own neurosis by calling trousers 'inadmissibles' or 'unmentionables'. And if they were unmentionable when worn by men, they were unthinkable when worn by women.

Of course, the idea that men have always worn some kind of bifurcated garment and women have always worn skirts is nonsense, as any anthropologist knows. Mohammedan women wear trousers. Roman soldiers wore a kilt, that is, a skirt; and so do the Scots and the Greeks even today. And in Old China all respectable women wore trousers. But in Western Europe,

at any rate since the Middle Ages, the bifurcated garment has been the mark of the male and the skirt the mark of the female; and this is obviously no longer true. Many young women today wear trousers as a matter of course, for work in the home, for shopping and even on social occasions. Even when, instead of trousers, they wear the mini-skirt, are they not repudiating their femininity? It might be argued that they are emphasizing it, as the female thigh is rarely as slender as that of the male, but it is the slender thigh which is admired, even by the women themselves. Perhaps we should accept the suggestion that the erotic ideal of today is androgynous. Certainly a slender girl in a mini-skirt bears the closest possible resemblance to a late-fifteenth-century young man in tunic and tights. And as young men are increasingly abandoning the formal convention of trousers, waistcoat, jacket and collar and tie, they too are adopting an outfit which might justifiably be called 'tunic and tights'. It would seem that the clothes of the two sexes are beginning to overlap, and even to coincide.

What then is the future of Fashion? We have tried in the foregoing pages to isolate the principles that seem to control it: the Hierarchical Principle, the Seduction Principle and the Utility Principle. In an increasingly industrialized and class-less society, the Hierarchical Principle is obviously in decline; and in a world of emancipated women, the Seduction Principle would seem to be shorn of much of its power. The Utility Principle is left.

And so we reach the stage—already reached in Communist China—where clothes show no distinction of sex and no distinction of class. And mankind, enlightened at last, can look back with pitying contempt on all those ages of Conspicuous Waste when men spent a lifetime carving an ivory balustrade and women ruined their eyesight making useless lace; when troops of workers, who might have been profitably employed building grain elevators, were toiling at the futile fretted roofs of Beauvais or the dark-gleaming windows of Chartres; when men strutted in silks and velvets and women preened themselves in satin and brocades; when the ends of the earth were ransacked for plumes and jewels, and the pelts of strange beasts; and mankind, having struggled upward from savagery to barbarism and from barbarism to civilization, saw itself as the Lord of Creation and akin to the Gods.

181

'Topless' Evening Dress by Rudi Gernreich, Los Angeles, 1966. *Photo by Erich Locker.*

Modesty in Dress

We, as children of an age which values equality above everything else and calls envy social justice, must congratulate ourselves that all these frivolities are no more, that Modesty has proved finally victorious over its two foes, the Lust of the Eye and the Pride of Life, that the Socialist Paradise has been reached at last, and Thorsten Veblen can lie quiet in his grave.

Male and female costume, 1966—no distinction of sex or class. (Photograph by Sally Soames.)

Bibliography

Adler, Alfred: *Individual Psychology*. New York, 1924.

Alexander, H. M.: *Strip Tease: The Vanished Art of Burlesque*. New York, 1938.

Allen, Agnes: *The Story of Clothes*. New York, 1958.

Allen, F. L.: *Only Yesterday*. New York, 1931.

Ballin, A. S.: *The Science of Dress*. London, 1885.

Barber, B.: *Social Stratification*. New York, 1957.

Beauvoir, S. de: *Le Deuxième Sexe*. Paris, 1949.

Bell, Quentin: *On Human Finery*. London, 1947.

Bergler, Edmund: *Fashion and the Unconscious*. New York, 1953.

Bettelheim, B.: *Symbolic Wounds, Puberty Rites and the Envious Male*. Glencoe, Illinois, 1954.

Binder, Pearl: *Muffs and Morals*. London, 1954.

Binder, Pearl: *The Peacock's Tail*. London, 1958.

Boehn, M. von: *Das Bühnenkostüm*. Berlin, 1921.

Bogardus, E. S.: *Fundamentals of Social Psychology*. New York, 1924.

Briffault, Robert: *The Mothers*. New York, 1927.

Carlyle, Thomas: *Sartor Resartus*. London, 1833.

Chalmers, Helena: *Clothes*. London, 1935.

Chartrou, J.: *Les Entrées solenelles et triomphales à la Renaissance*. Paris, 1928.

Compassionate Conformist, A.: *England's Vanity, or the Voice of God Against the Monstrous Sin of Pride in Dress and Apparel*. London, 1683.

Crawford, M. D. C.: *Philosophy in Clothing*. New York, 1940.

Crawley, E.: *Dress, Drinks and Drums*. London, 1931.

Cunnington, C. Willett: *Feminine Attitudes in the 19th century.* London, 1936.

Cunnington, C. Willett: *Why Women Wear Clothes.* London, 1941.

Cunnington, C. W. and P.: *The History of Underclothes.* London, 1951.

Davenport, Millia: *The Book of Costume.* New York, 1948.

Dobb, L. W.: *Social Psychology.* New York, 1952.

Donaldson, James: *Woman: her position and influence in Ancient Greece and Rome and among the Early Christians.* London, 1907.

Ellis, Havelock: *Studies in the Psychology of Sex.* Philadelphia, 1923.

Fischer, Carlos: *Les Costumes de l'Opéra.* Paris, 1931.

Flower, Sir William H.: *Fashion in Deformity.* London, 1881.

Flügel, J. C.: *The Psychology of Clothes.* London, 1930.

Flügel, J. C.: *Men and their Motives.* London, 1934.

Flügel, J. C.: *Man, Morals and Society.* New York, 1945.

France, Anatole: *L.Île des Pingouins.*

Freud, Sigmund: *Works.*

Fryer, P.: *Mrs Grundy: Studies in English Prudery.* London, 1963.

Garland, M.: *Fashion.* London, 1962.

Gernsheim, Alison: *Fashion and Reality, 1840-1914.* London, 1963.

Gill, Eric: *Clothes.* London, 1931.

Hambley, W. D.: *Tribal Dancing and Social Development.* London, 1926.

Hambley, W. D.: *The History of Tattooing and Its Significance.* London, 1925.

Hannay, J. B.: *Symbolism in Relation to Religion.* London, n.d.

Hawes, E.: *Fashion is Spinach.* New York, 1938.

Hays, H. R.: *From Ape to Angel.* New York, 1958.

Hildburgh, W. L.: 'Cowrie Shells as Amulets in Europe'. *Folk-Lore, LIII.* 1942.

Hiler, Hilaire: *From Nudity to Raiment.* London, 1929.

Huizinga, J.: *Homo-Ludens.* London, 1949.

Hunt, Morton M.: *The Natural History of Love.* New York, 1959.

Hurlock, E. B.: *The Psychology of Dress.* New York, 1929.

Im Thurn, Sir E. F.: *Among the Indians of Guiana.* 1883.

Jackson, M.: *What They Wore: A History of Children's Dress.* Woking, 1934.

Johnson, D.: *The Nudists.* New York, 1959.

Kirk, Ruth B.: *American Sun Bathing Association*. 1957.

Kohler, Wolfgang: *The Mentality of Apes*. London, 1925.

Krafft-Ebing, R. von: *Psychopathia Sexualis*. London, 1951.

Langdon-Davies, J.: *The Future of Nakedness*. London, 1928.

Langner, L.: *The Importance of Wearing Clothes*. New York, 1959.

Laver, James: *Taste and Fashion*. London, 1937.

Laver, James: *Letter to a Girl on the Future of Clothes*. London, 1946.

Laver, James: *The Changing Shape of Things: Dress*. London, 1950.

Laver, James: *Clothes*. London, 1952.

Laver, James: *Dandies*. London, 1968.

Lewinsohn, R.: *A History of Sexual Customs*. London, 1958.

Lowie, R.: *An Introduction to Cultural Anthropology*. New York, 1940.

Lynd, H. M.: *On Shame and the Search for Identity*. London, 1958.

May, G. J.: *Social Control of Sex Expression*. London, 1930.

Mead, Margaret: *Male and Female*. New York, 1949.

Merritt, Frances and Mason: *Among the Nudists*. New York, 1931.

Monro, I. S. and Cook, D. E.: *Costume Index*. New York, 1937.

Nicoll, Allardyce: *Masks, Mimes and Miracles*. London, 1931.

Nystrom, Paul H.: *The Economics of Fashion*. New York, 1928.

Oldenwald, R. P.: *The Disappearing Sexes*. New York, 1965.

Owst, G. R.: *Literature and Pulpit in Medieval England*. Cambridge, 1933.

Packard, V.: *The Status Seekers*. New York, 1959.

Parsons, F. A.: *The Psychology of Dress*. New York, 1920.

Pear, T. H.: *Personality, Appearance and Speech*. London, 1957.

Roach, Mary E. and Eicher, Joanne B., (edited by): *Dress, Adornment and the Social Order*. New York, 1965.

Richardson, J. and Kroeber: 'Three Centuries of Women's Dress Fashion. A Quantitative Analysis'. *Anthropological Records, 5. No 2*. University of California, 1940.

Róheim, Géza: *Animism, Magic and the Divine King*. London, 1930.

Rudofsky, Bernard: *Are Clothes Modern?* Chicago, 1947.

Shapiro, H. T. (edited by): *Man, Culture and Society*. London, 1956.

Sheldon, W. H.: *Psychology and the Promethean Will*. London, 1936.

Spanier, Ginette: *It isn't All Mink.* London, 1953.

Stekel, W.: *Sadism and Masochism.* London, 1935.

Stratz, C. H.: *Die Frauenkleidung.* Stuttgart, 1904.

Stubbs, Philip: *The Anatomie of Abuses.* London, 1583.

Taylor, G. Rattray: *Sex in History.* London, 1953.

Taylor, G. Rattray: *The Angel-Makers.* London, 1958.

Tertullian: 'On the apparel of women.' The Ante-Nicene Christian Library, 1899-1900.

Thomas, W. I.: *Sex and Society.* Chicago, 1907.

Vaerting, Mathilde and Mathias: *The Dominant Sex.* London, 1923.

Veblen, Thorsten: *The Theory of the Leisure Class.* New York, 1899.

Webb, W. M.: *The Heritage of Dress.* London, 1907.

Weininger, Otto: *Sex and Character.* London, 1906.

Westermarck, E.: *The History of Human Marriage.* London, 1921.

Wilcox, Ruth T.: *The Mode in Costume.* New York, 1946.

Winnick, Charles: *The New People: Desexualization in American Life.* New York, 1968.

Wundt, W.: *Elements of Folk Psychology.* London, 1916.

Wylie, Philip: *Generation of Vipers.* New York, 1942.

Young, A. B.: *Recurring Cycles of Fashion.* New York, 1937.

Young, K.: *Handbook of Social Psychology.* New York, 1960.